ON THE TRAIL WITH
LATIGO JIM
AND HIS
WONDER HORSE
RUSTY

JACK BUNTON
AND
REBECCA BUNTON

To order additional copies of this book, contact:
Xlibris
1-888-795-4274
www.Xlibris.com
Orders@Xlibris.com

ISBN: Softcover   978-1-7960-5514-6
        EBook   978-1-7960-5515-3

Print information available on the last page

Rev. date: 01/31/2020

CREDITS

David F. Latham
Editor of "the Montana Newspaper, Libby Montana
First issue dated May 11, 1989 thereafter until 1997.

Jennifer Mills
Thank you for organizing articles and keeping the
authenticity of the way Latigo Jim spoke.

Jack and Yvonne Bunton
A labor of love to tell Jims story and share his articles.

DEDICATION

This book is dedicated to my brother Jim Bunton, as you will learn to call him "Latigo Jim" his news paper articles are about a True Montana Cowboy and his wonder horse Rusty.

INTRODUCTION

This is a personal story about my brother Latigo Jim, the cowboy, who loved Rusty the wonder horse and lived in Libby Montana. This book is written just the way Jim talked.

The people around Libby and surrounding area loved Latigo Jims stories.

If you have the time for one more story, the richness of Latigo Jims memories will joyfully oblige. Jim and his wonder horse Rusty, upon whom many a tale is based, roamed the lush wildness surrounding Libby, Montana and "Became sort of a legend, kind of famous up in those parts".

Jim never learned to drive a car, he just rode his horse everywhere.

A women once said to him, "Geeze Jim, you dont drive a car, you carry a gun and you look like people did 150 years ago"

Rusty "loved his food, especially carrots, granola bars, raisins, and fig newtons," Jim swears that it was the garlic that made him so muscular and strong. But what Rusty loved most was "Going bye bye" with Jim, rambling and exploring with his best friend.

If you have time for one more story, you'll learn of Jims deer-antler hat band, the hiker who hoped to scare off a bear with a buck knife, and hundreds of adventures along countless trails.

"There were always three of us out there; the good Lord, Rusty, and me," says Jim and finally ends with a raised eyebrow, a grin, and "Happy trials and keep your powder dry."

FORMER MONTANIAN COLUMNIST DIES

By David F. Latham
Editor of the Montaniam

A former Libby man who wrote a column in the Montania for eight years has died in Missoula, MT

Mr. Bunton wrote a popular weekly column in the Montainian under the pen name "Latigo Jim" his column, "On the Trail With Latigo Jim". Appearded in the papers first issue dated May 11, 1989, and most weeks thereafter until 1997 when he moved to Missoula, MT

"On the trail with Latigo Jim was a collection of folksy recollections by Mr. Bunton of his life spent on horseback, especially the approximately 15 years that he owned and rode "Rusty"

The column was well known in Libby and Troy for its amusing misspellings and its closing line. "Keep Yer Powder Dry", was a local catchphrase for a time.

Latigo Jim died March 29 2011. In closing; Rusty the wonder horse was born 1972. Passed on in summer of 2003. Rusty died in his sleep, of no pain, no scars or diseases in his life, no injuries; physically or mentally. Take care and love your horse, work hard and you will have many, many happy trails as I and Rusty did.

ON THE TRAIL WITH
LATIGO JIM
AND HIS
WONDER HORSE
RUSTY

Latigo Jim who was born 150 years to late and rode his horse Rusty 38,400 miles through the back country of the Cabinet Mountains around Libby and Troy Montana.

I remember my brother as a quite man, loved Rusty and loved the solitude of the beautiful Montana mountains.

Jim would write me letters every day, he loved to write about himself and Rusty

And when they stopped, I called him up and ask are you sick or something, Jim said "No bro." thats what he called me I ran out of money and couldn't afford to buy paper. I went to the store and bought paper, envelopes, pens and stamps for Rusty year supply so he could write me every day.

At the end of every letter Jim would write,

"Im OK and Rustys OK. Oh by the way wife and kids are OK."

If your wondering about his name Latigo is a cowboy term and part of the saddle to adjust the saddle to adjust the cinch

As my brother Latigo Jim would say in his closing articles "Happy Trails and Keep Your Powder Dry"

Articles from the The Montanian:

(1) Was recalling one trip up into the high country a few years back, and to easily get up to my favorite trails, I was going up Cedar Cr. Road, well this one particular time Rusty and I got about a mile up the road, here's this car parkt right in the middle of the road! Odd? Yes, so I lookt for anything suspicious, I noticet nothing. But wait, I spotted a movement in the back seat, as I got closer, I seen and quickly lookt away. For there in the back seat was two individuals, one male and one female, engaged in a most uneak wrestling match! Which both usually come out winners, I hope anyway. Well, needless to say, Rusty and I moved on up the road. Rather hurrydly! And had a good day after that. Also, no more, er, ah, "bare sightings" either. Until next time, Happy Trails and Be well. Keep yer powder dry!

(2) I remember one time, coming back from town, I noticed some folks over at the wood carving stone where they sold wood carvings such as owls, eagles and such. The store had a porch with a front rail on it that was about three feet off the ground. I rode ol' Rusty over and said hello to a couple who had three kids about ages six, eight and ten. While I was talking to their mom and dad, they asked me if the horse liked kids and could they pet him? I said yes! Rusty loved kids and it is okay for them to come and pet him. As the children started over, I said, "Yes, Sir Rusty loves kids – he eats about three a day, and he hasn't eaten yet today." The kids suddenly stopped. Then I told them I was just teasing and Rusty would love to be petted. The kids began petting Rusty on the head, and then they slid down to his neck. All three kids locked their arms around his neck and begin to swing from side to side. Rusty held all of them while they were swinging and laughing. It was a good time for both the kids and the horse. Another time, a friend of my son, who lived across the pasture, was out mowing the lawn. Before I left to go to work, I thought I would go and say hello. Well, I started around the corner of the house when my son's friend turned off the mower. It backfired, "Pow" like a pistol shot. Rusty jumped a little, and I drew my pistol and threw down on the kid. The kid started screaming for his mom and dad to help him. As I put my gun back in its holster, I told the kid I was sorry, as I had thought something else might be going on. I had just acted automatically when

the mower backfired. It sure was the most interesting moment. It scared me, and I know it scared the kid – he was really shaking. It turned out that all was well, and we ended up having a good visit. Talk about your interesting times!

(3 – May 30, 1991) I was recalling one time, I was riding with a yung rider, since both rider and horse wher inexpierncet, I tried to show him what I do, in certain cituations. For example: one day we wher riding. His little mare laid her ears back at Rust, and made a motion ta kick Rusty! I told him, you should get after her for kicking! He ask how? For starters, I said, smack her with the end of your rains, soon as she lays her ears back, and hit her hard! Let her know you don't like her kicking. He never said anything. We rode on, a few minutes later, his mare started in again, this time, she got Rusty a perty good kick to Rusty's gaskin muscile! Rust just flinch a little – and kept walking. The fellow tapt the mare on the neck, then said, "Don't do that." I then said, "Hey, if you're not gonna educate that horse, Rusty will!" Well, we rode on, then it happened, his mare laid her ears back, and before she could kick, Rusty swung around, let her have it with one hind hoove in the side of that ole bitty, dern neer knoking her down and almost knoking the wind out of her. She composed herself, and the fellow said, "Gosh!" I said just Rusty teaching her a little respect! And that little mare was a nice horse (no more kicking anyway), after that. But that was our last ride together. I did hear that he sold the little mare and got out of the "horsing around" buisssness. Maybe it's just as well . . . Another time I was remembering after a long day's ride, with a couple of other guys, come time to part company, my friends headed south, Rusty and I headed west, towards Cedar Creek. As we left, I said goodbye, Rusty and I got about half mile away, and Rusty started a low, wine, whimpering type of whynny, I sware he was crying, because the other horses had to go home. I could not help but cry myself, for the pain Rusty was feeling. After I spoke and comforted him, he quit "crying," and we perceeded home. I was told once, "You better sell that horse, he will kill you!" How little they knew the heart of that big red horse named Rusty – my friend! Until next time, Happy Trails and Be Well! Keep yer powder dry!

(4 – May 9, 1991) How's your horse around kids? I was askt this, and I explained my daughter, yungest daughter, who is two, huggs Rusty's back or front leg! Also walks under his belly, and Rusty was as cool as a

cuekomber. This is not to say that every horse is. Many horses who are spooky or are abused, you do not want them around yung ones.

Just the other day I was currying Rusty down after our ride. Joyce and Little Rose was setting close bye. Suddenly Rose headed for the pump house. I stopt her then told her, "No! Stay out of ther!" Then I told Rusty to keep her out of the pump house, "Keep baby away!' A couple minnutes later, Rusty moved, put his head down, nuzzled Rose away from the door of the pump house! She tried again and Rusty poppt her on the head! She run to Mom un-hurt, but scared!

And she didn't try going over to the pump house, without Dad or Mom. Especially when the babysitter Rusty is around!

Happy Trails and Be Well! Keep yer powder dry!

(5) As everyone knows, Highway 2 was under major construction between Libby, MT and Troy,

MT, well for about a year. I and ole Rusty would wonder up and down the Hiway, wile trucks, scrapers, tractors and such zoomed around us, and Rusty not twitching a hair!

Well, the other day, one of the boys from the state hiway dept. stoppt, askt me not to ride on the hiway, for my own "safety," he said, interesting, how come it was not brought up about year ago?

Well, I told em, I will abide by his request and that I will not argue with em, but, if I have to, I will still go down this bye way. Law says, horse and rider has top priority to go any wher, under any cercumstances!

This law is about 2,000 years old, and still holds true to this day.

I'm not saying you should ride your horse into a dangerous situation, for isn't it dangerous just being on a horse? The law simple means horse came befor man, and man and machine. So law gives horse and rider, "Right of Way!"

Until next time, Happy Trails and Be Well!

(6) Have you ever broke bread with your horse? Rust and I have, many times. Oh, by breaking bread with your horse I mean, you take a carrott or an apple, and you take a bite, then your horse takes a bit, you take a bit, it takes a bit, and etc. till the carrott or apple is gone. Well Rusty's and

I most recent bread breaking was I sat down to eat my lunch, Rusty come over, nusseled my arm, oh, I said, want some salad (which I figured he would not eat). Well, I figured wrong. Munch, munch, we both polisht off the salad! Then I brought out my peanut butter and jelly sandwich, nussle, nussle, on my arm Rusty begged! So, munch, munch, he ate half my sandwich, I ate the other half. The next was my apple, I drug it out, I took a bite! Nuzzle, nuzzle on my arm Rusty went, so, we devoured the apple!

What price friendship? Love!

Until next time, Happy Trails and Be Well. Keep yer powder dry!

(7) I was told once I could take up any horse and ride him up ah bear's face and spit in the bear's eye. I was also told I was one of the best horseman ever seen, but I don't think so. Rusty and I are just doing our thing . . .

Also, some folks told me they heard the museum here in Libby wanted one of my guns! I don't know but as I told em, first I heard of that. And as far as I'm concerned, ya, they can have one, after I'm dead, and it's o.k. with my next of kinn. Otherwise, I'm keeping my guns, but if one gun is donated to the museum, is a nice thought, too.

I also heard that they will build a statue of Rusty and I, by the City of Libby, over by the band shell.

When I heard this, I said, the thought's nice I guess, but sounds like it could be someone wants something for the pigeons to set on! Interesting!

That reminds me, you know, I never mentioned (don't recal anyway) that Rusty never goes crap or tinkles in anyone's yard! Well he does not . . .

Only thing he left in 12, over 12, years is hoove prints. Spoiled ya say? Ya, I guess, but it's a nice kinda spoiled, ya gotta admit, I recal, one time, accurly, one of many times at somebody's yard or public place, well one time at Montana City Old Town Rusty was standing at the hitching rail. I was in the theatre, Rusty started whinnying, I come out, he whinned again, while looking at me. So, I said, "What's that matter boy?" Rusty then started dancing around! So I went over, patted him, then said, "Gotta go potty?" Rusty muffled out a low whinny, so I untied him, lead him out to the public road (Cedar Street ext.), Rusty took a dump, then tinkled!

Ther's a human in that horse suit, I sware . . .

A clean horse anyway. Rusty and I like that!

One time when he had a mare with him in the old pasture, she kept craping all over until Rusty kict her wile she was taken a dump, then went to the corner of the pasture wher the dung was pilled! The mare crapt ther from then on. That Rusty's a different breed a cat . . . ah . . . horse, for sure!

Until next time, Happy Trails and Be Well! Keep yer powder dry!

(8 – June 27, 1991) Was recallin' a couple of old memories with ole Rusty, about 10 years ago, a friend and I rode into town (Libby), and over to my place. We'd been riding for quite awhile so thought we would rest. Well as we layed on the front lawn, holding our horses, who we left saddled, and as we B.S.'t I told my friend how good I got ole Rusty trained, then I reacht up, grabbed the stirrup. Rusty jumpt a little, druge me about a foot, then stopt. Then I pulled myself up till I was in the saddle. Then I said, O.K. John, it's your turn! He said B.S., I'm not tryin' that. Eh, O.K. I said. No confidence.

But, to each ther own. The other incident was one day, I was in a mood, and I was up at the folks' place when just befor I took off for the high country on ole Rusty, Mom come out, askt wher I was going? I told her, then I said, look how well Rusty behaves and then I started poking

Rusty in the flank!

Rusty laid his ears back, motioned to me with head to "knock it off!" I said, Oh Rust, that don't bother you as I continued to poke him in the flank, he warned me again, but I continued to poke him, then he reacht around and grabbed my arm! I quit poking his flank! He let go, I then moved real slow, and in real "pain," I reacht up and patted him on the neck and said, it's alright,

I was wrong, you tried to warn me to quit, and when I didn't you made me quit. It's O.K.

Now! What's most uneak is that I can pat him in the flanks or accidently poke or kick Rusty in the flanks and just flintch's, but does nothin' else.

He knows! Horses (some horses), are most uneak for sure. So if you have such a good horse, do me a favor please. Give it a hugg. They will not take advantage I assure you.

Until next time, Happy Trails and Be Well! Keep yer powder dry!

(9) Do horses have a sense of humar? I'd like to think so recently I got kinda borred with the same old routine of feeding Rusty in the morning and at night, after riding. For years, same ole thing, so I figured Rusty was too, so one morning, Rusty come in, as useual, I came to his feed bowl, as useual, but this time I just shook his grain in the can, and didn't pour it in his feed bowl, and I walkt out (not as useual). Well Rusty came in, stuck his nose in his bowl, and as I watcht from around the corner, Rusty turned and lookt at me with the funniest expression on his face.

About that time, I come around the corner, laughing, and then I said, "Got ya!" then I put his grain in his bowl and patted and petted him and laught some more. I then went and had coffee wile Rusty ate his hay.

Well, I come back, I got my holster, noticet Rusty standing in the middle of the corral. Well, I came in the corral, his butt towards me, as I started towards him, he suddenly raised his head, **e**ars back, and backing up! I stopt, thought to myself, oh crap, he's gonna kick me! About that time, Rusty turned and walkt towards me, wynning to beat (expletive deleted), and come up and layed his head on my shoulder, all as if to say, "Got ya . . ." and then giving me a huggy! Then we went on our days ride.

To conclude: Do horses have a sense of humar? Well, I don't know about others. But I'm sure

Rusty does.

Until next time, Happy Trails and Be Well. Keep yer powder dry!

(10) One of the more interesting aspects of horsemanship, in having your horse do just about everything, is being able to shoot off 'em. I've had Rusty trained for this, but he must do a bit more! Not only should I be able to shoot off him standin still, but on a run aswell. And so, in a place (I will not disclose), but in the woods, I would take him, Rusty, through some manuvors.

First standing and shooting, at targets, then on the run while jumping a ditch then a log and shoot, rifle and pistol. And, as I've mentioned before, I urg you not to try this. Unless you know your horse, and your horse knows you. And has your every confidence.

I was once told I could take any horse and ride it up a bears face and crap in its eye. Probably so.

But that's too daring! Plus I'm getting too old for such things. But ole Rusty and I can still pull a few stunts if we have to.

That makes me think of a little pome I wrot. It goes somethin' like this:

Who is this person called a horseman?

Hair is sometimes grey,

His legs are crippled,

But he rides, he rides.

The value of gold is high, so they say,

But what is the value

Of all you survey?

Especially from atop your Appy, Palimeano, Soural or Baye?

And so he rides, and he rides.

Some call him a cowboy,

Some call on him to lend,

But one for certain,

You can call him a friend!

With mountains majestic,

And Prairies devine,

With God as his pardner,

And his horse and gun his best friend,

You will be seeing him riding,

Again and again.

Until next time, Happy Trails and Be well. Keep yer powder dry!

(11) One fine day my shoe'r said we should go riding together some time? I said sure, well later that summer, we got together, rode a few miles west of Cedar Creek, parall to the Hwy, then come back, then we decided to ride up to Cedar Lakes. When we wher just about to the trail head to Cedar Lakes, we wher talking about weirdos setting snares made to snare backpackers and horses on the trail. Well, we got to the trail head, started up it, got about 100 yrds or so, my friend and shoe'r was ahead of me a few feet when, "ker plop," Rusty went down on his front neese! I then though he stept into a snare, so I got off, bent over then I got stung! As I was figuring it out, Rusty now getting covered with yellow jackets, he stept forward, turned, come up alongside me, I then new we got ourselfs in a nest of yellow jackets. I hollard at Rusty to git.

He took off, but was interesting to note: ole Rusty was gonna wait for me to get on and get the blazes out of ther. Well, after Rusty took off, I followed on foot, looking like a wind mill swatting at them things, I hollard at my buddy to go get Rusty, he did.

All in all I turned out pretty good, because if my Buddy's hourse would have stept in that yellow jacket nest, his horse being a greener, would have probably killed my friend.

So I was glad that it happened to Rusty and me.

I got seven stings, Rusty took about 20 stings and bites.

Well, that's a couple a years ago, when that happened. I'm sure a lot of folks will rember it.

Ther was a lot of folks being stung. Also being thrown from horses that got stung. Interesting, but not Rusty. He's a realy good friend.

Another day as I went to feed ole Rusty his grain, I have to crawl through the fence near his feed boul, well today's a.m. feeding, I was having trouble getting through, so when Rusty seen I was having trouble, and on his side of the corral, he reacht down, grabbed my coat collar, pulled me through, and stood me up, then let go. I gave him a huggy, for this is what friends are for!

He ate his breakfast and we were off to our daily ride!

That's it for this week. And do me a favor. Hugg your horse today. Realy, it won't spoil them.

Great achievements can be made with love!

Until next time, Be Well and Happy Trails. Keep yer powder dry!

(12 – September 5, 1991) Was remembering a time out at Harron's Riding Accadamy, we use to go out on slow days and kill rattle snakes. When we got tired of that we would go catch some bull snakes and throw 'em in a rattle snake's denn. Or catch a rattle snake and throw 'em in a bull snake's denn.

Bull snakes are a good snake, none poison's they eat rotants and rattle snakes, rattle snakes ain't good for nothing, but killing people and live stock. If you don't know your snakes, its sorta tricky ta tell the difference, but if you look close, the bull snake, although colored the same as a rattler, but have not rattles, and are generally faster and longer. Generally just bigger than a rattler. Baby snakes we would avoid all together, for one main reason, baby rattlers look just like a baby bull, and are more poisons than an adult! But one snake was fun to play with was the garden snake (known too as a water snake). Like the bull, you can play with 'em and they love to be next to your body, and if, for some reason, one bites you, no poison!

Until next time, Happy Trails and Be Well. Keep yer powder dry!

(13 – January 24, 1990) As I recall, it was in the summer of 1983. I and ole Rusty headed for

Libby (the long way), up and around behind Plumber Hill, when I got about three miles from

Cedar Creek I heard dogs barking, the sounds coming from a clearing. So I headed ole Rusty up ther. We go up ther, no dogs! But did notice dog and deer tracks, we turned, headed back down out of the clering, I heard the brush moving on both sides of us, then in and out of the trees I saw four or five dogs, then on the other side, four or five more, as they darted around, they wher closing in each time they made a loope, so I figured this is a pack of kaenine that was probly chasing deer, so I waited till they closed to about 40 feet, then I sickt Mr. Smith and Wesson, and his six friends on them critters, I killed two off from our right, three off from our left.

Then as I was reloading, them dogs wher running away! Real quick. A good day's work I'd say.

Anywho the rest of the day went trouble free. One other thing Rusty and I have done for the first eight years when Rusty and I wher trodding around off and on. We would race the great Iron

Horse (trains)! I urge you not to do this, it is very dangerous. And too, I urge you not to try the many things I have afor mentioned. Unless, you are an expierienct rider, and you know your horse!

Then it is Risky, so I must ask you not to attempt such feats, but owning and riding a horse is

Risky in itself, so you are on your own.

In closing, what part of a horse makes up 90 percent of his agility, and basic good feeling, and mobility? If you said ther feet, you are right.

Until next time, Happy Trails and Be Well. Keep yer powder dry!

(14) I should have mentioned in getting acquainted with Rusty, one morning, I come out to feed

Rusty. After he ate his oats, he came over to wher I was, changing his water, and turned around and backt up to me. Well since he liket to have his rump scratcht, I started to scratch. He then shook his head, swisht his tail and then I figured his tail itcht, so I perceeded to scratch, wher

I found a tic. So, I perceeded to remove that with pine tar (hoove tar). I first figured to burn it out, but didn't want a horse running around with his tail on fire. Anyway, the tic was removed, Rusty turned around to me, and give me a big huggy, and went back to finishing his breakfast.

Then about two weeks later one morning he come up to me turned his butt to me. Boy I thought, not another tic. I started to scratch his rump (in case thats what he wanted). He shook his head, turned and lookt back at me, and nodded his head! Then I though, shit, it is another tic, so I perceeded to go through his tail, he pulled that out of my hands, through it off to one side and lookt back at me. I then said, Rusty what is the matter? He slowly turned, came up to me (broad side), and while standing within inches away (about a foot, I guess it was), he duckt his head, and let out the hardest kick I ever saw. Then he took off, stood about 30 yards away. I then said, it's

O.K., come hear, after calling him a few more times he came back over, turned on me. Threw his tail off to one side, I began to look down his hind end, and low and behold, here in the right cheek, a sliver, it was about two inches long, about an inch wide, embeded about an inch and a half. I then got excited and said, I found it Rusty! Rusty must of thought, boy this humenoide is sure smart. Well, while Rusty stood there, I got my jack knife out, slipt the blade between the sliver and his butt cheek, and jerkt. Rust flincht a little, I put some blue coat (dissenfectent) on it, he turned, gave me a big huggy, that was that. However, may I suggest, don't try this with your horse unless you and him or it are as close as two peas in a pod, then you would be wise to tie the critter. Rusty's a different breed of a cat. He whyishtae, friend, compondrae, brother . . .

Until next time, Happy Trails and Be Well. Keep yer powder dry!

(15 – June 21, 1990) In the winter of '79, as in many winters befor, I like to hunt cyotes, well this winter, Rusty and I got up on scenairy mtn., when I spotted a cyote on a side hill, about 500 yds away, I strolled old Rusty up to about 100 yrds. And the wylly crutter just stood ther, so I figured I'd better take my shot, I pulled my single shot rifle up, took aim, bang, misst! Cyote took off, I put the rifle up, grabbed my pistol, and me and Rusty hot doged it after this $75 dog ($75 per cyote pelt at that

time). Anyway, so when you are 1,200 pds. or so, and in about three feet of snow, and the cyote ways a lot less, you don't chase em for very far. So that was the one that "got away!"

The next enter prissing project for Rusty and I was meeting and working for the folks of Cedar

Creek Farm. I met Dan and Herb in the spring of 1980, when I askt for the job a care taking ther place, for them, more or less, adopting Rusty, they agreed. And the same arrangements, so far, it holds to this day.

Inbetween setting on the place, Rusty and I would go on ventures.

One time, we come to the place, folks who own it wher ther so we decided to ride on up to the old trapers cabins.

Well, the F.S. were building new logging road, and just off to our left, they wher working on a road that run pairalell to the old CD. Cr. Road. Well, I didn't know they were working over ther, and when we come riding by they toucht off a dynnimite blast, blew me out of the saddle, but not off old trusty Rusty, he just froze, I collected myself back into the saddle, and here come Dan and Herb yelling are you O.K.? I said ya. But the blast reminded me of the western movies ya see, but for me and Rusty, a repeat we do not wish to see, but if we do we shall endure.

Until next time, Happy Trails and Be Well. Keep yer powder dry!

(16) Summer of 1979, and Following Winter was not to exciting, but ole Rusty and I sure put on the miles, the first five years it was nothin' to cover 20 to 30 miles a day, 6 days a week, 4 weeks a month, 12 months a year, well mileage fer Rusty and I, figuring, an average of 10 miles a day, 6 days a week, 4 weeks a month, etc, from, Aug. of 1978 to Aug. 1988 we have covered over 30,500 miles. Many of them miles wher to Cedar Lakes, Scenairy Mountain, many trips to town, and up to the flats up behind the lumber mill, all starting out from Cedar Creek, then I've made a lot of trips north, up Pipe Cr., Rawlings Tracks, all round trips in a day, I believe in '79 I got Rusty uset to shootin, then I would ride by

a stack o' fence post, firin' turn an' fire again, hand gun first, long gun secund. Ole Rusty took to it like a duck to water. Yup, he's a good horse an' a good friend, too!

'Til next time, keep yer powder dry!

(17 – July 12, 1995) Won day last weak, after goin up good ole Cedar Creek, I thought I'd run ole Rusty up aroun the store. When I got to the parking lot, a lady on the poarch had a little dog on a leash. That dad-blamed dog started raisin cain, yippin and yapping. I thought fer a second that Rusty might stomp on him!

The lady grabbed the dog to shut its yippin. I said, "High." She reesponded in kind, then said,

"My dog has never seen a horse befor."

That's okay," I quipt, "Rusyt's never seen a toe biter befor neither!"

After a few more amiable politenessesesses, I said, "Good day" and went behind the store. But then Rust and me herd this yap-yap=yappin, and here come that little toe bitin, horse-hatin ball of fuzz. Forchunutly for it, its master was rite behind. The noisy little runt run around Rusty's massive hoofs, dragging its leash, until it finely succeeded in wrappin its leash around Rusty's leg. Rusty, bein the fine and easy-goin horse that he is, resisted the temptation to squash the varmint. Rusty just stood ther politely till the lady pict up her "viscous" dog and went on her way.

And after all that ruckus, Rusty and I got on our way. No hoofs bit and no little mutts squashed that day.

I was askt recentley what is the V-shapet thing on the bottom of a horse's foot extending from ther heal.

That particullar part of the horses anonamity is called the frog. It serves two perposes: One, it is a shock absorber, and Too: it is a blood pump to pump the blood up into the leg. Also the frog is a thrush warner (thrush is a hoove deseaze that if not attended to will cripple a horse).

14

If yer cleaning your horses feet and you detect a powerful stink, squees the frog. If thers no black ink oozs out, then just puex ther hooves! If ther is black gunk, call a veternearien and

Purex the frog right away. Purex will kill the backeria that causes Thrush. Ewell hav lots of headacke with Thrush if it is not checkt.

Had a "bizzy" day yesterday. We rode down to Cedar Creek flats, seen some kids and ther parents and visited awhile.

Wile at Cedar Creek flats, one of the kids askt, "How far do you ride?" I said, "Anymore, it's two to five miles a day. No 20-30 milers anymore but after over 38,000 miles in 17 years its time to slow down."

Thanks for askin, kid.

After that I had to get back to civilization to pick up my little Rose from the summer recreation program. From ther we went to Henry's Café fer cool bevrages and chatter. Nice place.

Then we went over to the Riddle Ranch to watch my freind Mark work a couple horses. He's a fine horseman and farrier!

Also, wile I was their I met the new owners of the Riddle Ranch. We had a fine visit and we seen some fine horsea. Ther was one not so fine, but, like people, thers always some knot-heded plugs in a bunch. That particlar "horse" will probly end up in a Alpo can. But better him ther than killing people.

And, as always, we spent part of the evening with Joyce at the Care Center.

Ole Rusty, that broom-tail scallion, he spent his evening muchen on grass, kickin back and takin it easy. Ah, the life of a pampered horse!

If yer sittin' there wonderin how me and Rusty do something in particlar, take a minut and write us a letter. Aisle be sure to reed it to Rusty for ya!

Right to:

Latigo Jim c/o Jim Bunton

316 Idaho Ave.

Libby, MUT 59923

(18 – August 23, 1995) The other day, me anda coupla friends, Lennerd and Tarry, went up to the outfitters to see how much itd cost to wrent a couple of horses. We found out it costs $125

EECH for 2 hours! Woe! Them bags o' bones are too spendy fer this ol' cowboy! That maid me realize what a grate thing I and Rusty have . . . and have had alla these years.

Just out of curiosity, me an Tarry and Lennard drove around to look at them $125 horses close up. While we was eyeballin them from the car, one sarol whinned, hungry (as they always are) but twas a good looking equine anyway, cepting for the price tag!

With that we headed back to check on Rusty. When we got ther, Rusty come down to the gate, and as Lenard and I talkt. Rusty come over and put the bumb on us for oats! He's a good ol' mooch! Butt in the process of Rusty's nuzzling, Lenard acted like he got nockt over! Dint phase

Rusty, tho, he just kep nuzzling. I didnt want Rusty's efferts to go unreworded, so I got him a can of oats to eat. Yum yum!

Then just befor we left I got a whole bunch of huggies from Rusty! I love it! And it didnt cost me no $125 neither.

One day last weak after Rusty ate his supper he simply HAD to have his bonnana, as sort of a chaser for his rashion of fig newtons that he had had erlier. Good food for horses, eh? Well, for Rusty anyway.

Recently I was askt, what does it mean when a horse has rings or little ripples on his hoofes?

Well sir, it could be a sign of founder. Look at the top of the hooves, about the couriniary band.

If thers a white puffy rubbery ring around the hind hooves only, founder is starting! If the white puffy ring is on all 4-hooves, then your horse is foundered! Just how bad only a veterneerian can tell. And a vet should be contacted right away.

Founder is real bad. Watch your hot feeds. Keep in mind, I'm no perfesssional or vet, but thanks for asking and may you and your horse be good friends fer many years.

Another one of my many frinds askt me, what kind of feeds do you feed Rusty?

Well, in summer it's 3 lbs of 3-way oats a day, with a healthy flake of alphafa, gras mix hay, and treats of carrots, raisins and fig newtons. Mind you, this is when he's not on pasture.

When he IS on pasture, I feed 3 lbs 3 ways grain. Standing just 2 lbs's. No hay.

During winter, it's about 6 to 8 lbs. of grain, and about half bail of hay. I try to watch his grain and alphapha so founder don't get Rusty. Also watch yer horses performance. If ther a good horse, and they start bucking and acting stupid, cut ther hot feeds, grains and alphafa. Too many carrots will hipe some horse up.

I don't give Rusty hardly any sugar, just what's in the fig newtons, and sugar mints, witch are few, and far in between.

Now since Rusty's getting older, I feed him a little equine senior. With his oats, also garlic once an awile. Voila!

One day many years ago while feeding Rusty his evening feed, my friends got a short ride on him after he ate. Just befor I turned him loose I gave Rusty a treat, and when I did, Rustys kallywacker dropt down, much to me embarrassment! One of the kids askt, "Hey, Latigo, whats that thing hanging from his belly?"

I said, "Thats Rusty spare tire. If one of his legs go flat he uses that one!"

The kid was only 3 years old so what else could I tell em??! Let his mom and dad tell em the facts of life when the time is right. And surly, they will have by now, I hope.

Boy, Rusty was havin a bad hair day the other day. We went for our regular jont, and when we got back, he started acting up. He's had a cough, and is geting old. So, I just got to take it easy!

Vet says Rusty's o.k. but when they pick up a couph one should take it easy on them. Plus he's getting old, too. He aint the spring pony he was 20 years ago!

Rustys up on Julie and Danna's pasture off an on, and when we get out ther, Rose goes and gets him. She leads him over to me by his main. "And a child shall lead them" it says in the Bible. I think its meant for people but works for Rusty too!

As Rose and I went up to Cedar Creek, she found an injured butterfly. She carefully pickt it up and carryed it till we had got home. On the way, in the car, part of its wing got broke and Rose started to cry, so as I confoted her, I said, "Don't feel sad, for this little creature is o.k. It's sool is in heaven wher dogs and cats go, and it feels no more pain, for its happy with God now. But always hold on to this feeling and carrying for the littlest of things and matters."

I was amazed that such words came from my mouth, because when I care taket the Cedar Creek farm, I became hardend and lost this gentle, compassionate feeling. In loving one thing, I lost loving for all things. But its coming back . . . I hope.

Well, I'm gettin tiery, better sign off. Keep your nose to the grindstone, keep yer eye on the ball and . . . Keep yer powder dry!

(19) Tooke Rose out on Rusty again thother day. When she went to get on Rusty she fell. Just a short way, butt a first for Rose. Irregardless, she wa'snt hurt is a cowboys way! She then got on, as ya gotta do in these sichewations, and ole Rusty was perfect.

He stood real still wile I got Rose composed. Rose is a trooper . . . shees tuph. Little cow girl.

From ther we had a good ride. Rose even found 40 cents on the trail we was ridin on, so it pays too "stick with it."

As I went about doin our daily chores coupla days ago, we – Rusty and I – decided to stop up on grandmas porch. So we did. I dint surprise Gramma none though, 'cause she always nose to ecxpect the unexcepted.

Later we rode on down to friends Bob and Sharals and spent the day. I hoisted ther little dog up on ole Rusty. It sorta like giving a kid a ride, don't ya know.

On our return to the coral, we run into Larry G. Davis . . . figuratively, of coarse. He was fine and wee gabbed about guns 'n' such, as uasal.

Wile we was over at grandma's roamin around, I said, "Rusty, you wanto loope?"

He jumpt and danct, so we did a little. But not to much . . . It ain't no good to loap with no shoes and no snow to run on. Goota keep Rusty's tootsies in good form fer our summer ecxurzions.

Was recaling a time when a fiend and I when t out gopher huntin. We seen an old roote celler, so we stopt and started to walk over to it. But as we got closer we smeled the unmisstakeabul rank stintch of bare! So instead of going in, we pulled our pistols and backt off slowly!

What a rush! We wanted gofers, but we didn't want a bear who coulda been gophering us! We did'nt axtually know if ther was one hibernatin in ther, butt it sure smeled like it! Woulda been interesting if we woulda walkt in ther! Ther might have been alot of shootin for sure! Ooh wee, boy!

Well, until next time, you be sure to stay outa trouble. Don't sass yer folks, clean yer plate and keep yer powder dry! An if you fell like writin a letter, go ahead. I'd like to here from you.

(20 – September 27, 1995) A coupla weeksa go we went down and seen them Budwiser

Clydsdale's at the shopping center. After viewin them, it ochres to me that I wold not want one of them steping on my foot.

Afterwords, Joyce, Rose and I and Joyces friend Jenny went over to Heritage Musium. Quite a place them volunteirs have putt together. We got quite a bit of heritage and rellix in our area. Its good that someone is keeping track of 'em.

The next day Rose and I road our pal Rusty up up that Cedar Creek Rd. We seen two snakes and white tail doe. Rose realy liket that. After our wildlife adventure, we stopt to check on getin

Rose a rabit, sents she's bin wantin' one so bad.

While we was ther, a nabor come over an dropt off some tools. He had his dogin his van an it started raising hell, barkin and scufflin at big ole, quite, gentle Rusty. Some kids come and tried to quiet the mutt down, but dint work. So the fellow finaly come out and yelled at him and he finely shaddup. I commentated to the feller, "Yer dog minds perty good, and thats good! I was thinkin about quietin him down myself."

The fellow said with a snort and a snear, "You stick yer hand in that van and yule draw back a bloody stump!"

I retortelated, "Oh, I wasn't gonna reach in with my hand. I was gonna reach in with this," and I showed him my 38 sic-shooter. The fellow jus kinda grumbled and got in his van and left. Me?

I just chuckled. I guess he didn't want his mutt getting a bit of lead poisoning!

After our incounter with the yappin dog, Rose and I road Rusty back to the barn. After a short cool down period and a quiet huggie, Rose and her little buddy Justin swung on ther barn swing.

Now usually when they swing back and fourth, they bump and codle Rusty, and uasally enjoys every minute of it. But this time, Rusty was laying his ears back and glarin at the kids. So instaed of rough housing, I just fed him and put him out to pasteur. He mite be getting a littel old fer that kinda stuff. Ain't we all!

Well, I had a happy horse, but dissapointed kids. Oh well, they'll get over it.

I was askt, how do you tell a horses age? By ther feet? Buy there ears? By their tail?

None of them ways, that I know of. Me, I guess the horses age by ther teeth. At five they gets ther bit teeth. Then you can tell a lot by the angle of ther grazing teeth. Thats what I do.

Someone told me once that wen a horse eats, he grinds off his teeth a little each time, so that by the time he gets real old, he aint got no teeth left! I dont no if thats true, BUT . . . if you go to buy a horse and he has dentures, look out!

The other day Rose and I was gonn go have supper with Joyce at Libby Care Center, so I askt

Rose to go get cleaned. Wile she was in currying herself, Donna Davis, Larry G. Davis's wife, came to pick us. But Rose was still not ready! I hollard, "Rose you about ready?" "Just a minute," she replied. About that time, she come out, snuck in the kitchen, got a bandaid and put it on her chin. I askt, "What happened?" She said, "I cut myself shaving!" "Oh my goodness," I said, "lady's don't have to shave their faces! Just wash up and you'll be alright." Ha! I know she wants to be like me, but shavin??! No sir. Not now, anyway. She'll get plenty of shavin in when she hits 60!

Well, I gotta go and contemplait our next exsgursion with Rusty. Say, I sure do like hearin' from you out their in readershipland. If you feal like writin, drop me a lime.

Keep yer powder dry!

(21 – April 2, 1995) Ole Rusty is feelin bedder since the weathers warming.

Wile he was eatin his breakfast the other day. I notict Smokey (the Cat, not the Bear) was not around, so I said, "Hey Rusty, whers' Smokey?" A minut later, Rusty lookt towurds the maine house. Bout that thyme, here comes the barn cat, Smokey.

I figger them animals got sum kinda Inn Tuition. They jes watch over each other.

Shortly thereafter, Rusty and I headed out for our daily ride. We went to grandma's an pickt up her male, then ambiled on down the Hwy. You mighta seen me out there by Ceedar Creak bridge. If you do, wave. I've waive back.

Befor we quit for the day, I notict a long piece of plastic hanging from the gargage dumbstor. I grabbed it, pulld it out with my cain and put it back in the garbage. Funny thing, ya no, sum horses are fraid of rufflin plastic! Butt knot Rusty!

Last weak, I took our duahgter Rose out to give her a ride on ole Rusty. She loves him muchas I do.

Rose played on the hay in the barn, then played with Smokey the barn cat, wile Rusty was enjoying his meal of hey. After that we road up Cedar Creek, checkt the old deer carkus for kyotes. I told you bout that in won of my earlier calumnies. There wasn't no Kyotes to bee seen, so we went and got grandma's mail – as always – then over to Floyd's wher we chatted awile.

Wile chatting ole Rusty cockt his head, looking behind hymn, so I turned and here was Rosey laying flat on her back on Rustys rump, playing with a flashlight I gaver, taking it apart! I told her to set up, for that was no way to be riding a horse. Could be dangerous!

An important lesson learned for Rose: never lay on a horses rump to dessassembulate yer flashlight. Ya might fall off an git trompled.

After that hare-raisin incident we called it a day and headed for the barn.

Took Rose out again for a ride a fyou days later. After Rusty aight, I took him over to the stairs I use to get on him. I reacht for the stirrup and mist! Butt Rusty thought I connected, so he stept out. I said, "Whoe, whoe!" Rusty stopt. Hee's a good horse.

I said, "Back up, Red." He backt up. Good horse. I then cought the stirrup, got on. Phew!

Quite an operasion just to get on my big, fore-leged buddy!

Rose then got on and off we went. We maid the uasal rounds . . . mail, dear karkus, Hwy. ect.

When wee got back, Rose wanted to jump off, so she did. But me, bein not quite so knimbull, I took the smoothe weigh off . . . when Rusty an I got to the barn, I slid off his butt. Nice and easy.

Rose went to play on the pole gate and fell off, kerplumph! Nothing hurt buy her dignity.

Imagine that! After a day's ride, Rose gets buckt from the pole gate!

Well, all in all, a good endin to a good days ride.

With that I leave you with this: Watt is a horse's vision at knight? Quite good, ackshually! Its about the same as you and I see on early morning or evening hours. So don't try to sneek you up onna horse at knight!

The other day after makin the usual round, I took ole Rusty to a nabors for a lope across their field. All of a sudan, Rusty was wanting to buck, more of a crow hopp! Awnry fart!

The nabor was not home so we went on down to Cedar Creak store an lopet across thier parking lot. Their was a big dog in the back of a pick-up there, and he started to bark at us. I reacht fer my gun, a sic shooter, but dind't need it because the dog wized up and backt off.

From their, we went up CD Cr. Rd. to sea if the road was still closed. It is!

On the way back, three pups came up a runnin. Once come in front of Rusty so I goosed him . . .

Rusty, I mean. The pup run off then came around infront again, so Rusty took the inishitive! He put his nose down and put the run on the pup. That did it fer them pups! Off theay ran, over to a nabors to romp and play. Rusty and I just watch em rompin fer a minut, then I said to Rusty,

"Ah, to be yung and rompin again, eh? Shure is neet to watch the yuth enjoying life, sewing ther whiled oats. To quote some famous person whose name escapse me: If youth only knew . . . if age only could!"

On that note, I leav you with this reminder; Horses are oat powered engines. Do not step in the exaust!

After riding the other day, Rusty wanted in the barn, so I let him in. Know reason not too!

I then workt on the saddle stand for awile, as it neaded some ajdustments. When it come time to head home, I went in to the barn and told Rusty to scoot.

"Time to de-barn," I said. So he did. I grabbed some extra hay for him and put it outside. He began to eat, butt then he started to throw the hay around, so I pickt some up and put it back.

Then Rusty cought it with his nose and tosst it! Thus began our grudge

24

match, punching back and forth with a handful of hay. Finaly Rusty gave in, and wisly so. Never bite the hand that feeds you the hay!

Rustys getting to be a bugsy little twit in his old age. But he's still my big ol' Red buddy. When you got a freind – horse or otherwise – you take the good with the bad. To conclude, how many hairs are in a horses tail? Not enoulf to swat flys anyway.

One day last winter I met a hitch hiker on Hwy. 2. I chatted with him for a tad. He was headed to Kalispell so I suggested he stop at Becks Café, probly get a ride ther. Don't know if he did. If you see a guy standin' there, that means he didn't!

After that Rusty and I went on up Cd. Creek, behind Cedar Creek Store. There's still snow and ice back ther. As we went, we come on a drainage. There was ice just befor it, so ole Rusty step on it, crunch, then jumpt. We plowed snow for awile then we called it a day. Was a nice ride, but I think ole Rusty likes a little grain, yeast and raisins with his ice.

With that, Happy Trails and Be well. Keep yer powder dry!

P.S. You kin wright to me with your questions bout horses, or ridin, or other such things. I'd sure like to here from you.

(22 – July 5, 1995) One time at the Libby Café when Joyce was workin theer, I popt in fer a cup.

A friend of hours come in and we said, "Hello." Then I askt, "Hows your little black?"

"Shees fine," he said, "but I still cannt get her to neck rain!"

So I askt him quizichially, "Jew every try a runnin Martin Gale?"

"No," he asid, "she's right outside, want to ride her?"

I said, "Ya, I'll try her!" So out wee wint for a tryout! Ooh, fun! I got on her, grabed the rains in a G-hall position and started her out. She fought it, so I pulled her up and tryed juss neck raining her, and, by crakcy, she started working fine!

N fact, I blieve she neck rained fine from there on! Yup, ya just gotta trane em right from the starret.

Speaking of Cafe's remids me of another cafe wich had a sign that read: "Dinner special!

Turkey $3.25, chicken or beef $2.25, children $2 and double!"

At another I saw, "A Super B and inexpensive restaurant. Fine foods expertly served by waitreesesses in appetizing forms!"

A frienda mein, Mrs. Keith Williams and her littel girl, Rashal, gave me a ride out to visit ole

Rusty, so I showed him of a little. I stood nexxt to Rusty's face and pealed his eye lid back so they could see his eye ball! No Visine for him! Just my dusty ole finger!

I then cleaned his ears with my finger to show em waht a REEL was buildup looks like. Then I run my fingers up his nose! Gotta get the buggers out!

Then – the "piece de resiistance" – I put my gloves on his ears! Ha! Just call me, "Dr. Jim,

ENT!"

But most of all the little gal liket petting Rusty soft nose and feeding him fig newton cookies.

After my ride, and befor we headed back to Libby, I rattled off all the horse parts by name. Not much exitment, but pleasing a little girl in her first association with a horse. And especially cause her first association was with the best dang horse that was ever rid . . . Rusty!

Question for ya: What is the frog of horses hoofs used for? Answer next year . . . ha ha! Just kiddin!

The frog's uses is 2-foled: 1) as padd, and; 2) to pump blood up into the leg. Interesting thing this thing called horse.

I was recalling a time a few years ago when I went to Montana City Old Town – the deefunct tourist trap at the end of Cedar St. Ext. in Libby. I was lettin Rusty graze with his bridal on, and he stept on his rain. "SNAP" went the bit in his mouth! Hmmm, I thought, thats cool! I'll never get another bit in his mouth. So I askt Joyce to go get a hackamoor. She did, and I put it on without too much trouble. Then I put in on Rusty. Ha! Just kiddin'.

Wile I was rideing Rusty with that, he was getting to free headed! So, I got a bridle, held it up and Zap! Ole Rusty put his head right in it. After that, Rusty was doin his grazin with a holter on, or nothing at all! After the bridle thing, he confined hisself to giving kiddy rides on the boardwalks of old town!

I was askt recently, "What is the longest ride you vever been on?"

The longest ride of my many rides was the 30 milers! One time I rode to a point up Pipe Creek from Cedar Creek, witch was about 34 miles! Long rides! Good times.

Me and a friend went out to the rifle range to burn some powder and bust a few caps and a spray can. He was shootin his new pitstol and I was shootin my carbine. He shot his pistil butt was not doing so good. Course when ya get a knew handgun it takes some time to get use too it.

Well sir, he askt me if I wanted to shoot his little 45. I said yeah, and I started bouncing that spray can all around. But befor that I had bin shootin my carbine and could not hit my mark! So my friend took the carbine and shot, and he was doing real great. Should of askt if he wanted to trade guns. But I was never any good with a carbine. My handgun expurtease comes from years of practice, and practice, and practice, then practice some more. And if you take this practice to a horse, then ya get perty good!

All in all, it don't help when its cold out and ya get the shivers, but we did perty good. Was a good day. Especialy keeping your eye sharp in the shootin game.

Well, I had better sign off now. I don't want to get riders cramp.

If you fell like corresponding with me about any horse madders, you kin right to me.

Happy trails and be well! Keep yer powder dry!

(23 – April 26, 1995) Went out to feed Rusty this a.m., and I saw the sighed of his head was all bluddy. Upon closer inspectation, I foun he had clipt his ear on somthing, plobly barbd wire.

Then blood was runnin down his face! Most dramatical!

Well, I cleaned it up an gave him a huggy fer good measure.

We saddled up and went up Cedar Creek looking for bear, or sign of some. We did find some bear scat on the road about one and a half mile up Cedar Creek Rode. But we never seed a bear, allthoe we lookt hi and lough.

With that Rusty and I came back an rode over too grandma Junes fer a brief, "How Dew," then we went hot dogin over to the store.

Not much their, so we hot doged it over to Julies place. But no one home! Humph! So thenn we rode over to Jack's old pasture and Rusty moed what grass theyr was and I munch on my luncht. Muncheon on Luncheon . . . Hay! Perty good!

Then I and Rusty loapt up to Marvins wear we seen my daughter Leasa and son-in-law Dean.

The kids wanted to no about a trail that goes up to wher the fire was last summer, so I told em bout it, insofar as Rusty and I had logged many miles up that particular root.

By then it was time to call it a day. So we did.

I have been askt, wher was the first horse come from? Well, God actualy. But your first known breeds wher Arab's. I don't know what them things wer that was running around in dynasour days, but the way I learned it, all your horses today come from Arab's. I could be wrong, but . . .

The other day when I went out to feed Rusty, I found hymn to be in quite a mood. He was running and bucking, "feeling his oates," as they say.

After he was dun goofin off, he come and ate. But wile he was eatin his hay he got a piece of hay stuck in his tooth. As he was trying to work that out of his teeth, his eyes wher rollin around, makin him look kinda crazy. Sorta like Ben Turpin. Mmember him?

Well my frind, it started pourin down rain so we didn't ride that day. It was a good monsoon comin down, so I come home.

Later that evening wile I was down at Libby Care Center vistin Joyce, I run into Marlen Heried, the juj. We had a good visit. Marlien, you was askin about my surgery. It was from an ulcer.

And no, its not wise to ride a horse after belly surgery. But I jus cain't seem to stay off ole

Rusty! Me and hims are ridin feends!

Also, to the lady who complimented me on my last Latigo Jim colum, again I thank you. I am very happy folks enjoy the readin as much as I enjoy writin em.

29

Also I think she said sheez a late reader, so if I may recapitulate: I have rode Rusty over 38,000 miles; weave chaset bears; hunted together; racet the train; we been through a dynamite blast together; three forest fires. So you kin see, Rusty an I are quite the team.

I've been persuaded to tell of the time I administered first aide to a yung ladd who was hit in the temple with a rock. I was later tolled that without the first aide, he coulda died.

There was also one time when I helpt a fellow who was in a car accident west of Libby. These escapades may sound heroic, butt theyd plobly do the same fer me if they were in similar circumcistantses.

Oncet I was askt to go out to Pipe Creek to help a friend guard his ant's place. When we got their we had to run off a bunch of drugies! I didn't figure I was comin back from that one! But we won ot. Right makes might all and all.

Most important, God knows, and documents, the good you do in this life. But you don't wanna get too cocky, or He'll put ya in yer place!

Coupla weaks ago Me an Rusty and Rose went out, rode back to a place whers thers a natural spring. We took a few slurps, then we come home and got on the grey mule (that electrified, three-wheel rascal) and went up to Asa Wood School ground to Rosey could play. Then we went up to Henrys and had a treat.

On the way back we got to goofing off on the grey mule, spinnin brodies and doing twistys, and we got dumpt! A good fellow came by and helpt us up. I wish to thank that fine gentleman again for the help after our wreck out front of Asa Wood School.

Last Sunday, after Lonny Kelly dropt Joyce off after church, we had lunch, then Rose and I hoockt moms weel chair up behind the grey mule (that rascal) and off we went to Asa Wood

School playground. Wile Rose played on the toys and junk, I pulled Joyce around doing weelys and whippy dos. Joyce was laulphing so hard, think she wet her britches!

After that we headed for Henrys Café for coffee and worming up, then it was back to Asa Wood for moore phisacle vehicular entertainment. Maybe I kin figger out a way to get a wheel chair fer Rusty so he could join us!

Well, my friend, I'll keep my eyes peeled for you as I mutate around town. If you see me and Rusty, or Me an the Grey Mule (that rascal), be sure to wave!

Happy trails and be well. Keep yer powder dry!

(24 – March 22, 1995) Met some new folks, Bob and Sharals folks. Sharls mom and dad. Like us, they like a good rodeo, so we have been meetin at Bobs home, and watching rodeos and movies, and vistin. The reason I'm writing this mainly is they have a real good guard dog, and ain't to many people it takes a liking too! But it did me. Witch I have not found a dog yet, that didn't meet me half ways. They seem to know if ya have evil in your heart.

Resently I come across some two-headed headlines in papers. Thought I'd pass em on: "Squad dog helps dog bit victim." O.k. How about this one: "Miners refuse to work after death!" No kidding. Anouther? O.k. "Autos killing 110 a day, let's resolve to do better." Say what? One **m**ore, o.k. "Mrs. Corson's seat up for grabs." Hmmm, they are talking about election? Last one: "20 year friendship ends at altar!"

Went down to the American legion for a brandy and 7-Up with boy Nate and daughter-in-law

June. Well, we got our drinkxs and got some tunes on their music box, and then Nate and June started playing a little pool. They askt me if I cared to play, so I did. Not bad iether, but would rather play Polo instead. Butt all in all, it's a good game, this thing called billiards. Er, pool, I mean.

Went out to feed Rusty the other day, then we saddled up. Since he was looking down the other end of the pasture with that "whats that down ther?" look, after Picking up grandmas mail, ole

Rusty and I went down and lookt for his "spook!" Found no spook, but did find some elk dung, so Rusty had company, a horned bull, or prety cow, at any rate, Rusty did not want any part of iether but was telling me "somethings down ther." Witch is good.

From ther we went on down the track, seen some B.N. boys working on the R.R. tacks. The siad they wanta take the tatie-tatt out of the train when it goes over it. So I said, take the tatie-tatt out of the rail, so the train don't go boom budie-boomb, huh? They said, yeah! Try to, anyway.

From ther we rode over and seen Floyd, good nabor, who had a black Labratory dog pesterin him, so Rusty and I drove him home! Then after a jawing session with Floyd we, Rusty and I, called it a day.

Oh, that remines me. I'll leave you with this. "The dog ran across the lawn, emitting whelps all the way." A final one, on table manners. "It is bad manners to break your bread and roll in your soup."

Was needin a ride out to feed ole Rusty, so I got on the phone to swop shop and my buddy Rojjer

Sheelds. Right after that, Sharal called me and said her husband Bob would be glad to run me out when I needed too. So he has, and A couple days later I invided them and ther yungins to come on out and I'd give them a ride on ol Rusty. Yesterday I gave them each a ride, and during each ride, mom and dad would take snap shots with a flash camera, sometimes within about a foot from ole Rusty's face and Rusty doing nothing but twitch an ear. Then Sharal got on and wrode Rusty a bit, then we quit. Then was time to go on home, so huggies wher given, even to the kids.

To conclude, if your horse is not use to Mr. Kodack and his flash, I would not put em in your horse's face!

Happy trails and be well! Keep yer powder dry!

(25 – April 12, 1995) Well, my frind, it was a perty usal day today, ecceptin when I fed Rusty his evenin meal. Wile I was in the barn forking up hay, Rusty stood at the barn door with a look on his face that sed, "kin I come in and help?"

So I said, "Shure! Come on!" So he did. He done a little janitorational work on the barn floor, cleanin up, eatin the left overs. He's perty tidy, fer a horse.

I'm writing this from wher I got a good view of Rusty's belly. Don't try this at home! Yew might git a kick out of it.

As I sat down to write this the wend blue the barn door against a folding chair sat up outside and it maid a sound like a knocker. So I said, "come in!" Rusty lookt at the door but no won come in. I could see him thinkin, "Musta bin the spirit people, I guess."

Rusty and I headed em up and moved em out this morning with a clippity clop ride up to the mudslide on Cedar Creek Rd. We made it up to the "rode closed" sign.

Lass time we was up their, I had tried to prop up the sign with my caine, but it slipt outa my hand, and I coulnd't reach it. Then today, there my cain was, hangin from the sine and within my easy reach. So to the person who reset the sign and hung my cane on it, I thank you very much! Montana is sure fulla good fokes!

From ther I rode over to Cedar Creek up behinde the Cedar Creek store. Rusty and I sat and lookt at the creek fer awile, listening to the bubbly sound. Then we come out behinde Woodys

Trailer Park and road towards Rustys barn.

We gott to the Cedar Creek store parking lot, and here was a yung lady in a perty dress. Shee stopt and askt me what the name of the creek was? I said Cedar Creek. Two lakes feed it from about seven miles up from Hwy. 2.

A fine day and a fine lookin yung lady . . . specialy when the wind was blowing! Oh no! The cowboy in me is coming out!

Looks like spring today, but with the wind and snow it seems moor like fall.

Rusty and I went up an old loggin road today. Was up hill allot of the way, mighty steep, but old horse and I ploud right up to it. We found that our detour around the mud and downed trees blockin Cedar Creek Rd. was also cut off by downd trees! So wee turnd and headed towards home. But first we went over to grandma Junes fer a short "how-dee-doo."

At daze end, I give ole Rusty a huggie and held onto his neck. Then I said, "lets have huggie for mom!" He huged!

"Lets have a hugg for grandma!" He hugged!

"Let's have a huggy for Jim Jr.!" He hugged!

"Now one for Leasa and family!" He again hugged!

"And one big one for Bob." Done!

He hugged a big one for Nate and family! And a hugg for Mike, too!

"Don't fergit Rose!" One more Hug.

"Oh, wait, Rusty, one for me!" A big one was given! Feels good.

After all them huggies, Rusty lookt at me an said, "finaly! Now I get to eat supper!" But he loves his huggies just as much as his grain and all.

Do you know what a hore'ses greatest fear is of? If you say falling, youer right!

Rode into town and stopt at Mr. Russell's Conoco gas station. Filler up? No, we just for a drink of water. Then we rode over to the new Liby Biulding Suply at old Cash and Carry. We watcht em build on that fer awile, then hedded to the feed store.

Fellow come out, said, "looks like you knead a knew saddle?" I said, "Shure, but know can dew!"

Aftr ole Rusty and I finish our B.S.ing we headed back to Cedar Cr. On our way we seen Pastor

Frank of the Christian Victory Center. They wher just comin back from seein the Kootnai Falls.

I told em how once I pondered tryin to take Rusty across that swinging bridge, but never tried it.

I'm sure Rusty woulda went, if I coulda got him up them steps!

Now I leave you with this: Watt does it meen when a horse's ears flop down? It means the horse is showing discomfort, oar ailing.

Happy Trails and be well! Keep yer powder dry!

(26) Ole Rusty proved ta be a dweeb again, as I probly mentioned befor. Aftr a day's ride Rusty gets a bath. Well today was no different . . . well, almost. Ordinarily, I turn him loose. I go turn on the water, then after I call him 30 or 40 times, he comes, and I give him a bath. But today, I called him, he didn't come. Then after the fourth call, he whynned! I said, "No oats till you get a bath, you know that!" He whynnd again! I said, "No! Not until your bath! So, get over here!"

Perty soon, here he come with a long, powty face, as if to say, "Gee Boss, why do I have to take a bath befor supper?" So, assuming that's what he meant by his expression, I said," Come on, a clean horse, is a happy horse!" Well a bath was given then his supper given!

Days end . . .

An interesting happening today with ole Rusty and me. I was late getting to his feeding, so as I approach Rusty's barn stall and started in, he stept back, then reared up, ears laid back, front hoofs thrashing out in front. Neet. As I stood ther watching, I thought of the wild horse, and in ther way, most uneak.

Ah, Spirit . . . may it never die. Big red horse, getting old but still got the sass.

Anyway, it was a long dogy day, just one of many, in a cowboy's way . . .

Until next time, Happy trails and Be Well.

Keep yer powder dry!

(27 – January 31, 1995) One day hear recently my friend and family drove Rose and I up to

Elko, Canada, for a day drive. Sumthing different, and different it was! Just on the other side of

Libby dam, heres a heard of moutin sheep. Got with in 10 ft. of them. They was all rams an I was a lamb.

"Ah, Rusty, round em up!" I new I should of brung him along!

Wile at a cafe at Elko, I seen some folks order raisin pie and ice cream! That reminded me of a story of raisin pie witch I'll pass onto you: This little gal wearin a mini skirt was waitressing in cafe an this yung fellow came in and sat down at the counter. Little gal askt, "Waddle you have?"

Guy says, "what kind of pi do you have?"

She says, "lemon, banana cream, co-canut cream, punkin, mince meat, and at the very top of the pie case is raisin pie."

He ordeuvres the raisin, so she gets out a stool an stands up on it. Butt shes still a little short, so she hasta reach for the pie, and when she does, her skirt comes up. Well, she cuts the pie and puts it back. Bout that time, anouther yung fellow comes in an sees "The show." Well, he sets down. She askt, "Whattle you have?" "Oh," he says, "I'll have some raisin pie." So agian she gets out the stool, stands on it, reachin for that raisin pie!

Bout that time this old man walks in and sets down at the counter. The little gal steps down, slices a peace for the yung fellow, then looks to the old man and says, " I suppose yours will be raisin too?"

"Oh no honey," the old fellow says, "mine just (CENSORED UNDER PROVISIONS OF

MONTANA'S PROPOSED OBSCENITY LAW, HB 83) a little."

Well, I told the little Canadian waitress that one and we moved on back towards Libby encountering them mountain sheep again. Really neet, and a fine trip. Thanks Robert and

Charee. Was interesting.

Went out and fed old Rusty thother day with my son and grand kids. While Rusty was eatin, little Sahara, my grand daughter, was huggin Rustys front leg, until dad and grandpa got after her to not do that. She might get a kick out of it.

After awhile I saddled up ole Rusty and noticet that he responds even better now than befor to voice commands under saddle. But out in paschure he only does what he wants, no matter what ya say to him. But I follow our old catch up routine, and he respondd. Today in leaving, small gate come back, hookt him under his flank and back leg. He stopt, lookt back. I hookt the gate again, gave it a shove, and we left. And got our chores done, two!

Just the other day, Rusty proved to be the same old Rusty (trusty Rusty, a friend once called him!). Anyway, Rusty and I finish our daze chores, an I was tired! So, I thought, before I fead the old boy, I'd set down a minute. Well, next thing I knew ole Rusty was nuzzling my arm, wakin me up! I said, "Huh? Oh, O.k. let's eat." All the time he was knickering, I just said, you better not be a cussing me! Or I'll run your bunns up to Cedar Lakes.

He quit knickering!

The ansure to the horse chin whiskers question is: The horses chin whiskers are used to tell the horse what he's grazing on or eating, along with its nose and eyes of course. Now, the question fer next time: What is a horse nose whiskers used for?

Happy trails and be well! Keep yer powder dry! And I don't mean yer baking powder, neither!

(28 – January 18, 1995) Ole Rusty got a Roomie for a short time resently. Fellow came along

Hwy. 2, stopt and said his horse was lamed up. He askt if he could put im in with Rusty. I said o.k. so they put the little mare next to Rusty's place in a small pasture.

So Rusty had a little lady come calling, but could do no courtin, what with that fence in the way.

Just as well, though, cause she lookt tired. Guess her and her master been travaling cross country, so best to leave courtin to another day!

I been feeling more better lately. Since the weather has wormed a bit, I thought ole Rusty and I would get awile. Butt by the time I got saddled, I was cold! The gall durned gall bladder operation took more out of me than I thought, so I told Ole Rusty, "it's a no go for today!" I unsaddled Rusty an turned him loose. He went over and snuggied up to the mare, then lookt at me sorta snorty, as if to say, "I wanted to stay with her anyway!"

So, I said, "I know ya'd rather be pichin and whooing, but tomarrow its supose to be warmer. If so, we ride!"

He came back over and give me a huggy anyway. Sure miss riddin every day. Wheel do it again soon.

Puzzul: If it takes one guy to paint a house 3 hours and another man 5 hours to paint a house, how many hours does it take both men to paint a house? I figured 8 hours, my boy said an hour and 74 minuets.

Do some figuring, I'll tell ya the ansure later, according to the T.V. anyway.

Got ole Rusty out yesterday an went and got Grandma's male. Wile ther at the mail box, Rusty started his crying, low whynie, because the master of that little mare took her away. Rusty hadda touch of heard fever. I just said, "it's o.k. big horse, told ya they wher coming to take her away!"

He dint answer.

Well from ther we rode over to then around grandma June's, then we rode over to meet some folks from Alaska. Whilst talkin to them I started to eat my raisin, peanut butter an jam sandwitch, I give Rusty half so's he woold quit whining bout that mare. Well, he ate and quit whineing.

As we sat talkin, I pulled my cane off the saddle, as if in a charge position. He, Rusty, got set . . . of course, he may have though I was gonna bop him for bein a geek about the mare and teasin them Alaskian kids.

Inn concollusion: How do yoo ride a horse with no shoes on ice in the winter? Very carefully!

One day, after saddling up Rusty, I went to put his bridal on. I held it up an said, put your head in hear! So he did, and that reminded me of a story: ther was a foreman on this here ranch . . . a

Dude Ranch, it was. They would get a bunch of dudes to pay to come their and learn to ride, rope, roundup cows and etc. To start, they would have to catch up ther horses, witch whur on the green-broke side. So the foreman handed them each a larriet and said, "don't mess with that sorral with one white sock and the star on his four heard. He's my horse."

"O.K." they said, and out into the corral they went to "catch ther steed!" Well after chasin them horses around awile and catchin nothing more than air, the foreman says, "What's the matter with you guys??! Catch them horses!"

So again the dudes tryed, again catching no equines. The foreman says, "When you guise gonna quit foolin round?"

So a couple of dudes turned and said to the foreman, "If yer so smart, lets see you catch your horse."

"O.k." foreman says. He grabs his Larriet, steps out away from the coral fence, makes a big loope in that rope, and whistles. Ole Big Red comes over an puts his head in that loope, then just stands ther!

"I got my horse!" the forman says. Maid them slickers feel like dopes!

Well that uneak group finaly, FINNALY, cought ther horses. So then its time to saddle up and get to work!

When they got ready to go, the fourman took off into a lope, and since the dudes seen him take off, they kickt ther horses into a lope too. Butt since ther horses wher a tadd bit on the wild side, those steeds took off bucking! The forman stopt, lookt back and hollard. "When you boys are dun clounin around, the cows are in this direction!" I don't spect that they learnt too much bout ridin' during ther short visit ther.

Dudes come, and dudes go. But learnin horses and such kin be very interestin. And by the way, do you know what the whiskers on horses chin are used for by the horse? Ansure in my next calum.

The other day wile riding, I was wonderin if ole Rusty was still worth his salt. About that time, I come up to a rode that crosst the rail road tracks, then I heard the big iron horse coming . . . choo, choo to the yungins, deasle train to you modern folks. Anyway, wile the train was passin over the R.R. X'ing, I pointed ole Rusty at the train and we ran write at it, till I pulled him up and we stopt about 2 foot before hitting the train! Fhew! I said, "Ole Rusty! You've still got it."

Well, the next day after some chores, I set down in the coral to eat my lunch, and here come Rusty. Hmmm, I said, what to feed a pal! Ya know, friends gotta break bread together. Ah, a fig newton cookie. Ole Rusty ate 3 of them. Then he started to lick my hands, then my head (my hat on my head, I should say). "Yes," I said, "I know ya love me!"

The horses I've rode befor wher good, and ol Amar was great, but I gotta admit, that ole quarter horse Rusty is the best.

Happy trails and be well! Keep yer powder dry!

(29 – December 1994) As a lot of local folks know, the summer of '94 was not only hot butt very dry, and ther for we had fires. Seems like all over fires was burnin.

Well, one day, word come down I had to avacumate Rusty from Cedar Creek to a place up down south of Libby. Well, we got out ther and got settled in shor torder. Nex day, I took Rusty out fer a ride (boy was he glad to get out). Ya see, he was kep in a reel small coral an he was ready to go! Out!

Wien we got out, we went! That ol horse would realy get out and boogie! I was woried couse alla the smoke in the err, but no harm done, faraz I kin tell. We feel o.k. this winter.

Anyway, Cedar Creek did not burn this summer, thank God. When the evacuumation notice was more or less lifted, Rusty and I went back out. He an I are thankful no one was killed. Ther wher a few injuries I heard, but not bad. An to all the firefighters, we say, "Thank Ewe. Wee love you and God bless."

Was recalling resently bout won time while the Hwy. 2 construction was going onb, Rusty an I rode up too a guy who had a funny car. 'Tad buttons on the car dors nsteada handles. As we **t**alkt, I askt, "what kinda car is that?" He said, "its all computerized!" "Oh," I quipt. "Howds it work?" Sow he said, "auto start!" The car startd its own engine, all buy voice command!

"Boy," I said, "they done come along way scents the horse and buggy days!" Course I figured the car was computoreized but I wooda thot ya had to push buttons to operate it. But voice command!? Come on. I figured he had a remote gadget he punches out a comand in sequence numbers behind his back computerized car, then sez, "auto start." Butt, it had ta be, because he was no night rider with a car named kit!

Ah, the moderon age, isn't it wonderful? Well, in some ways, eh?

Was talkin to the pastur of our church on the phone. As we talkt, the subject of havin a

Christmas tree came up. I toled him I recald how Rusty an I would go get a Christmas tree for those who could not go get one. I never had and still don't have the money to buye such things for folks, so ole Rusty and I would go out, cut a tree fer such familys and bring em in, the old fashion way. Twas fun. And felt great. But can't do it anymore.

Went out to feed Rusty next day after talkin to the pastur. Rusty came out hot-dogin it and buckin and kickin! He come runing buy me, I grabed my caine, pointed it at Rusty an said,

"here." He turned and run away then come walkin up real slow, "wanting a huggy," so I stopt.

He lookt at my cane, approacht me slowly, put his head on my shoulder. I said, "I know son, you rember kickin me, but took ya long enoulph to apaligize? Yer lucky I didn't have my gun!

You realy made me mad when ya kickt me in the leg, and only 4 days after I got outa the hospital too. Ya geek! So now, all is well. I forgive ya," I said. But still, ya gotta watch em horses, esepcialy older horses!!

Had to run my yungest boy over to Boners Ferry Idaho to pick up his gear from a job he was on.

We stopt at a cafe, I got to talkin to a little gal who was waitressing. She said she had 2 horses, an Appy and a Morgan. One was one and a half and a 5 yr. old. The waitress lookt to be about

25 or so. I told her I was from Libby and had a quarter horse for over 16 years. An then I askt,

"how far she had rode her older horse yet?" She said 20 miles, I said your yung yet. Me I've put over 34,000 miles on ole Rusty in over 16 years. And have chaste bear, racet the train, been threw a dynamite blast an 3 forest fires, hunted on ole Rusty . . . she interrupted, and exclamated,

"over 34,000 miles! What did you do, count the miles?" I said yes. You count em. 20 to 30 miles a day, 6 days a week for the first 5 years, 10 miles a day for about the next 8 years. 2 ta 5 miles a day for the next 13 years, you add em up.

"Wow," she said, "thats alot of ridin." I said ya, if ya gotta horse, do not let em sit. Is bad for them. Her eye brows whent up, and she shook her head up and down.

With that we left, an I wisht her Happy Trails and Be Well. Keep yer powder dry!

(30) Just recently, while setting in the barn, waiting for ole Rusty to finish his hay, when I recalled the first horse race I was in. It was also when I was finally aloud to ride usin a saddle!

Well, a bunch of us from the acadamie went to the spur tavern, the horse I pict was named

"Patsy," a mare, well, I thot it was because she was a she! Well, the line was formed, we would race to the corrals, just about 100 fee befor the corral, the boss's son would flag the winner!

Well, Bang, ther off! We wher off and racing, we come roaring up to the boss's son, I was in the leed, the boss's son waved his hat, Patsy spooked, almost jumpt out from under me, but I glumed on! She run to the corral and when she stopt, I was half on her side and half under her belly.

And about a foot off the ground, so when she stopt, I just let go. "Plop!" Unscared! But I found out why every body called her Patsy! It wasn't because she was a she horse! It was because she played all the riders for a patsy!

I rode Drifter after that, unless I had to work the kiddy corral!

Until next time, Be Well and Happy Trails. Keep yer powder dry!

(31 – July 20, 1994) Was remembering when goin up to a place, not far from Rusty's pasture, 3 boys, all brothers, they askt, can we have a ride on Rusty? I said sure. So won at a time I'd give them a ride, then they askt if they could come down to the barn? I said sure, while down ther the older boy noticed a B.B. gun I had in the barn, he askt to look at it, I said sure. After looking at it, he said I'd like to buy it, I said sure how much, the askt. $7 I said. Well, the boy said, I'll have to get the money, I said o.k. when you get it, you can have the gun.

Justa few days later the barn was broken into, B.B. gun was gone. So I did some investigatin, and it all come up to yung boys I knowed so I confronted the boys. They said they did not take the B.B. gun, I went and talkt to ther dad, he said the oldest boy (the one who wanted to buy it), had brought it home, told his dad he bought it, I said no he took it out of the barn! His dad askt him, the boy confesst, said he took it. Well I told em, give me the gun back. And I'm willin to ferget the whole matter. He got the gun, and his dad said for him to work it off for me, but he never did.

So one day I come riding down by ther place, 3 boys done come out, "Kin we-uns have a ride on

Rusty?" I said sure to the 2 younger brothers, and to the oldest I said, no ride for you boy, for to error is human, to forgive devine, and I forgive ya, but I don't reward thieves! And don't be hanging around the barn neither.

As the old saying: Hurt me once, shaime on yew; hurt me twice, shaime on me. Enaulf said.

Went out to feed yesterday morning, Rusty came around then went to a big tree by the barn, then lookt down pasture, so my friend said, hey, Rusty's looking at something, I lookt, didn't see nothing, I said, nah, he's just fooling around until I get his grain. Then we heard a dog yipping, as we lookt down the pasture, I said, thers a dog down ther! "Ya," my friend said, and it sounds like it's trappt or snared in something! I said, you could be right, then Rusty walkt over to the fence of the north side of the pasture and stood looking, I said, Bob, you want to walk down ther and see if thers a small dog trap of the pasture and stood looking, I said, Bob, you want to walk down ther and see if thers a small dog trapt or hung up in the fence, he said sure. So, he did, short time later he came back, said thers a little dog hung up in the barb wire, he said, "I'll go get my gloves and go back and get it!" I said here, take mine, he did then Rusty wanted to eat his oats, so I fed him. And I told Rusty, thanks for telling us about the dog.

A few minutes later, Bob's wife came down and her girlfriend went down and some time later, they came back with a Pekaneez type dog, when I seen the dog, I told them it belonged to folks up in Cedar Creek. So, they said they would take it back up ther.

A good deed done! Thanks to my Rusty, a friend, and his wife and girlfriend.

Was remembering my first huntin trip on ole Rusty, I got on the trail, of what I lookt to be a good sized elk, so up in through the timber, of some fresh dropings ther, I told Rusty, then after running into a whole maze of tracks, I pickt a set and followed them till, I lookt around and, holy smoke, I was lost! Well I continued huntil till, I figured to blaze's with it,

I turned Rusty around and said, "Go home son." Rusty lookt around for a minute, I also gave him his head, he started back.

Some 3 hours later I notict familer ground, then I said, "O.K. boy, I know wher I am, we go home," I took the slack out of the rain and away we went.

Lessen! If yer out in these good old piney woods on horse back, and you get lost, turn your horse loose, he will bring you home.

Until next time, Happy Trails and Be Well!

Keep yer powder dry!

(32 – January 15, 1997) Got the barn roof shoveled off, thanks to Latigo Jim Jr. and the

Cincanati kid and a nabor. Now, it looks like it had never been shoveled off.

What a winter, beets anyting I've seen since 1964.

I was askt, they see horses with holsters on them, why is this?

2 reasons, 1 the horse is'nt broke! Or the horse is hard to catch. At any rate, don't go around them unless you have the ouners permission.

Also, I'd like to know what you folks are doing to get through this winter without going bonkers?

I know you yung ones are probly making whoopee! Luky devils, but what else you all doing?

Just courious, I know yer shoeveling a lot of snow but, your indoor time?

I've been writing a little, reading and watching TV, hoping the weather'll warm some so ole

Rusty and I can get out and ride a little.

Also I would like to ask those of you who see birds out forging for food, or dogs or cats could you feed them? It don't take much! Thank you. And may God bless you.

Rose and the Cincanati kid got kinda spookt about Rusty, they was wondrin if he might run over them? So he askt, will a horse run over you? I said no, you can stand or lay down in front of a horse, or a stampeding herd and they wont run over, or even step on you. But cows will! They will tromple you. Its known you can put a baby on a wild mustang and the baby will be unharmed.

Also on a related subject, the Cincanati kid told me he took his daughter to a local zoo in

Cincanati, and this larj bird came and took the donut that his daughter had had, the kid wanted to chase that bird down and get that pastry back, but that that that he had had had been eaten!

Huh?

Was askt: Does horses at anytime have all four hoofes off the groun? No, at any gate, they always have at least one hoove hitin the ground.

But it sure looks like, don't it?

As we attended Rusty and Smokey's breakfast thother day, the Cincanati kid shoveled snow, and how! On his break, we chatted. Then, he needed some change, so when he brought his wallet out I pulled my pistol and said, I'll take your wallet, so he jerkt the money out and handed it to me (the wallet). Very funny I said, I put my gun up. He put his wallet and money away. And then he went back to work, then it was time to go to Henrys fer java.

Say, my hay is getting low, anyone has a spare ton of hay. Could you give me a call? Thank you.

Got out to ride yesterday, was great, the weather was warm, went up to

Cedar Creek Rd. found it to be pluwed all the way to the trail head by work of mouth anyway, well wen I got out to

Rustys, with the Cincanati kid, I got Rust almost all dresst when I realized I forgot my bridle, so

Rusty had to wear his holter, course he is always good, I hardly ever hafta beat him.

I was askt recently, do horses talk? Yes they do, but not like Mr. Ed of TV fame. They talk with their bodys, ears back is being mad, pawing is hungry or wanting to lay down, kicking at stomack is they are having a tummy acke or colic. Food drulls from the mooth is saying they need their teeth floated (filed), tail swishing is just at flys or nervouness. Ears forward is attn.

Ears flat is disromfort. Eyes crost is drunk. Layin flat is sleepin. Cold and stiff is dead. Ha!

Happy trails, my friend. Keep yer powder dry and your frogs wet.

(33 – December 25, 1996) This here is a copy of a pome wrote by my amigo Jack R. Estes of

Corvalis, Oregan. I'm sharon it with you cause I think it goes perty good with Christmas.

The Tree at Christmas

The Tree at Chrismas is apropros

Just how it started we'll never know

The sparkling tinsel brings forth surprises

From the one-year-olds dear twingling eyes

We speak to find it, the reason why

Its presence raises our hopes so high

Fair fragrance spilling like rare perfume

Pure beauty thrilling the joyous room

See how the branches reach out to all

Warm firelight gleaming from ball to ball

Oh divine spirit from up above

We thank thee for the tree is love

The tree at Christmas, we love it so

Gaily wrapped presents, bright lights aglow

Keen sleigh bells ringing across the snow

Sweet children singing carols below

Our snomans growing so big and fat

Right now, he's wearing old grampas hat

That feeling grows with each yule season

Everyone knows love is the reason

See how the branches reach out to all

Warm firelight gleaming from ball to ball

Oh, divine spirit from the above

We thank thee for the tree is love

Infinite spirit, pure sacred dove

Bless all your children with perfect love

God bless you Jack, this be our Christmas wishs to you all. Merry Christmas and Joyous New

Years!

(34 – November 27, 1996) Winter of '96 is proven to be an old fashioned, Rocky Mtn. gut shivering, snow bound type of winter, temps ranging from 0 to 30 below "round here."

Anyway, in feeding the old big red war horse (a.j.a. Rusty), he still got the spunk, even in the snow and cold. Ever day when we get to the barn, ole Rusty comes up behind me and starts rubbing me on my back, like to say, "I love you, Jim, but hurry up and feed me! It's cold!" So I always give him an extra rashon and a treat, plus the obilgtory Huggy. Then it's back home to cabel TV and warmth!

Wile I been hold up in my oun castle, I oiled my saddle (don't tell Rusty I said that. He thinks its

HIS saddle) and reogonize my desk. Its been a reel mal function jungtion lately.

My son Bobs Army recrutor stopt by to give Bob some papers, but Bob wernt here so we chatted awile. I told him I trained Rusty like the old calvery poneys wher trained. Lots of ridin and shootin at the same time. Rustys used to it now. Heck, he nose guns better than most people!

Hepful hint: wile out in the cold. Don't breath and move quickly!

I never wrote about when I moved Rusty into the McGrady place. That was about 1990.

McGradys is on hwy. 2 near the Cedar Creek store.

About four months after we moved in, a big grey house cat, Angora, female, spadeded, moved in with Rusty. Joyce, my bride, calls her Smokey. The name stuck!

Sometime later, a Road Island red roaster moved in, witch I call Roaster Caggburn. Hes cool.

Hes a good watch dog, er, rooster. Betwixt him an Smokey cat, therye good companions for

Rusty. And Rusty takes good care of them cause he thinks hes a human.

One time Rusty was chasing Smokey for fun. Smokey stopt real quick and Rusty had to pussy foot around to keep from steppin on him, but he was careful not to.

Quiet a wile after we moved in, a duck (not a wild duck) moved in too. I noticet it had a hurt wing so I gave it some 3-way oats and a warm place in the hay. Then one day it come wadalling out and lookt at me as if to say, "Hey I'm outa here. Thanks for everything!"

I said, "Ready to go eh!" Then it took off and whooshd away in that funny quick flaping way ducks fly. I'm real good with animals and I'm sure he said "thank you" as he flew away.

Shortly after the duck, a cute little pig moved in. I figgered I'd better find the owner, since cute little pigs turn into great big fence breaking hogs! I checht around and found the owner. They come and got it. Rusty acted like he was real sorry to see that porker go. Not me!

After all the livestock shuffling, I told Don McGrady, "All we need is a couple of cows to move in and we would have duck soup, chicken and doumplins, pork and beans and beef for winter!"

He agreed, but he reminded me that my diet don't call for such friskasie. So we just keep em for company, for Rusty. He likes it.

The chicken and Smokey and Rusty are still at the place today.

After old Don died, his place was boughten by Mr. Stanford (Spike) Lewis. He's a real fine fellow. When he moved in, Smokey, Mr. Caugburn and Rusty gaive hime a warm Montanian welcome to Libby. Spike was so touched by them that he's letting me keep em ther on the place.

He likes horses and animals, and Rusty, Smokey and Mr. Coggburn are easy to like!

Thanks again, Spike. Whinny. Meow. Cockadoodldoo.

Happy trails, be well, keep yer powder dry.

(35 – October 9, 1996) Rusty! My compondrai and kemosabee! The Cincanati kid, bad Roy, askt me if I wanted to go camping I said sure, so we went up to Bear Creek found a spot wondered on down to the creek sat, had a beer, and talkt, then drove on some back roads, in going down this cows trail I call it, all of a sudden heres vast rock quirry so I started to study it, when all of a sudden, about 20 feet from the truck, the ground moved, something light tan, for the second I saw it, it lookt to me to be a grizz! He big bad dood, the Cincanati id, back the truck up, stopt, got prepaired for a jont, and walkt down to wher the great furd critter had been, sure enoulf, here was grizz droppings! He come back up, I took his picture, he told me of the poop down ther, lookt to be of what I described early as grizz poop, so, must have been a furd critter called the grizzly bear, so I tol him, I got his picture, and I'm gonna tell every one yer the best grizz poop inspector, cheaf inspector of grizzly poop! Well, it was back to camp and to set up we did, and the great kid did all the setting up, for being an Easter tin horn, the kid is all right.

So if ya see a 1994 Blue Chevy pick-up with shell camper on it, give hime a wave, but he still can't shoot a shotgun and hit anything.

Course, I won't touch that riot gun for nothing! Give me a horse pistol any day!

Happy trails. Be well, God bless, and don't take any wooden nichles. Keep yer powder dry.

(36 – October 2, 1996) Just resently my son asked me how many horses I rode befor Rusty. My anser? Fort-teen, and most of 'em I road at Herron's Riding Acaddamy. Ad to that the couple I road here in Libby: Coa Coa, Trigger Happy, Yahee and and Amarr.

Then I got me the best horse ever . . . RUSTY!

I started riding when I was bout 16. But now with my bunged hip I don't do too much ridin cept for short rides up Cedar Creek on Rusty. Mostly I ride my old gray mule, that rascal!

I figure Iv'e rode Rusty 38,000 miles more or less. I don't know how many miles I've rode the other horses, but I'd gesstimate that I've rid about 65,000 miles total. On horses, I mean.

If yer constimplating riding horses as a carear, be prepared: I'ts a hard, cold life, always in the saddle, sore butt, sore legs, not much sleep, no money! But no worries, neither! And the coffes good!

I was down to Henry's havin coffey the other day and I run into a guy who has some appalousas.

We got to jawin and he told about one time when he saddled one of his appys up and it fell over!

He got the saddle off and in about ten minutes the horse got up. The feller was wondering, What hapend?

I assomd his horse was in good shape, so I askt him if he had tightend the sinch up reel good. He said yes. I said well, their's your problem.

I ecxsplaned to him that there's a artery that runs under their girth that floes blood to their front exsteemitees and brain. When you tightin that sintch up reel tite, it cuts off the blood flow to that appys brain and BOOM! Down it goes! Lights out!

I told him, when you tighten up the cintsh, make sure you can get your fingers under them latigo straps. This will assure you happy trails and no hard landings!

You may've noticet that my calum has'nt been in the paper lately. Thats cause I nearly stopt writing it. The calum. The editor said he was'nt sure if he wanted to keep printing them. I tolled him I thought a lot of people like readin it. He said he wasnt sure.

So, dear reeder and good friends, I woold appreciate it if you'd write to the editor of the

Montananian and let himn know what you think about it. I like tellin you my storys and Ive herd that you like readin them.

You know, my old Rusty horse is 24 years old. That's about 80 in hunam years. In his old age,

I'm careful to worm him about twicet a year. I use Zemectrin paste wormer and three cloze of garlic sporiodically throughout the year. He stays pert healthy most of the time.

I regelate his feed accordion to his neads. I can't ephasise enought the importance of making any changes to your horses feedin habits SLOWLY. Sudden changes in Rustys diet can give him a belly ache and flatus, which hurts us both!

Allso, don't feed your horse any sweets. Their teeth'll rot just like humans. For treets, feed em carrots, sunflower seeds and such. Apple bits are okay too, but not too mutch.

Its getting to be winter, so be sure to take your horses shoes off. The metal draws the heat outa there legs into the cold, cold ground.

Well, gotta go oil the grey mule, that rascal!

Keep yer powder dry!

(37) Went down last weak and brought Joyce home from the Care Center. I towed her home in her wheel chair behind my grey mule, that rascal. Was sort a fun, Joyce a swiveling to and fro, dodging traffic and hitting pot holes.

We made it home alright and sat in the back yard awhile, enjoyin the after noon, something we had never did done befor. Now we do it all the time after my ride on Rusty, per Joyces wishs.

That reminds me: Last week Rusty and I rode up Cedar Creek and seen some fresh black bear dung. Must be spring. No see em though. Fact, we seen no other fur bearers either. Was a fun day. Course everyday above ground is a good day.

I was recently askt, do horses have a pole? Yes the top of the neck along the main is called the pole!

I was talkin to Rusty the other day about summer. He says he likes summer cause he can lay down for as long as he wants and not frieze to the ground. And he's not to partial to thick ice in his troff. Makes it mighty hard to get a drink, and that CO-O-OLD water brrrrr, it freezes his nosstrills and his pree-hensival lips . . . he said.

I said, "Rusty, don't you even like ice water in the SUMMER? Or ice tea?"

Butt he just layed there and didn't say much. I think he was ignoran me. But he lookt good there in the tall grass. Cool too.

I was thinking maybe on his birthday in July I'll sneak out a big bag of ice an dump it in his troff, just to full him! I want it to be a surprise so don't you tell him.

Well, I better go and check the battery terminals on the grey mule, that rascal. Keep yer powder dry!

(38 – February 1996) Went to feed Rusty his poney chewins thother day.

It was colden a which's teat. Ol Rusty din't like it. That 20 below stuff is for the birds, not the horses.

Afetr I had feeded Rusty an give him a good talkin' too, me an my tranporter hopt in the jalope an whizeed into town. I said lets stop at Henry's Cafe so we did. I seen my Friends Dave and

Carol Latham. They sure wher dresst sharp. Dresst for Funzies at St. John's Hospital is good, fund raising deal anyway. An' it gives the Lathams an excuse to put on them funny closet. I can't wait til the hospital has "bikini" day.

Well after visiting at Henry's over a steemin cup of jovva, I and the kids Billy Edwards and

Joanna, left. Upon pulling up to the innfer section of Hwy. 2 and Idaho, the light turned green for us, so Billy started threw the intersection.

"Whoe," Bill I and Joanna said, on your left, zam, here come a van, with a uneak Libbyite driver.

Bill hit the brakes and we stopt, and he, who almost did not pass hiss driving test, swerved and went around us.

Now to him, and all the other uneak designated drivers, I just have these final words: Hurting or killing them kids and giving my car a big owie, is the worst thing to happen, BUT, kill me, and itll be no more On the Trail with Latigo Jim.

So, at any rate, please be carful wile yer on the trail, thank you. My kids, and Rusty, and Snoopy and Smokey and Mr. Cougburn thank you too!

I and ol'd Rusty are sure glad the whether is gon for now. We was getting perty tired of bustin' the troff ice ever day. Gimme spring any day, when I kin just git a drink any ol time I wisht. But don't pet yer long johns away yet. Ol' Pukestuffonny Phil seen his shadow the other day. Six more weeks of winter!

Happy trails and be well. Keep yer powder dry. And warm.

(39 – April 1996) My latest, most recentest birthday was kuwite a day! It's the day I foaled 52 years ago! So to sellebrate, after feedin Rusty his morning chewins, my frind Roy and I drove out and around an up and over Bear Creek Rd. We snoopt around, din't take no pichers thouhg, cause nither of us brung a camer. Butt we joyed ourselfs looking for bear, tigars, snakes an dother sich deelectables.

After we had consummated our peregrinations (them's a couple words the editor put in . . . I would a just said "got back") we stopt at the Pionier Junktion Cafe, just south of Libby on Hwy.

2. Roy had a cinnamon roll and coffee. I myself had a fish sandwich in a piece of paper and a slab of apple pie with a candle in it. Mmm mmm mmm! Bes tasting candle I ever ate!

Before I blew the candle out I made a wish: For good friends and for good health, for these are true richs in life. Yupper, if you go threw with one good friend, yer fortunate.

I have 4 grate ones: Den Hinkle, Larry G. Davis, Roy and Rusty. My wife and family are held in a special way. Thanks to all for an especialy great day. God bless you.

And I could of kisst that perty little gal that waited on us. She was cuter then a Derringer and sweeter then unsulphured sorgum cakes.

Yessir, This has been one of the best birthdays I've had. And all my friends make me look forwrd to even more, future birthdays.

Later that day, as we was approaching Rusty during our coming out to feed, Rusty was putting the bomb on us (Roy and I and Rose)! Well we got his grain to him, then muncht on his hay wile Rose swung on her swing. I and Roy just chatted between mouthfuls, then come time to go,

I and Rose got our huggys (of the horse type, not the dispozable diper type). Rose got her first

(ladys first ya know), then I nuzzled up to my pal Rusty and got a big long huggy. As I started to leave, Rusty grabbed my coat! I turned to see watt he wanted. He let go of my coat and pointed his nose towards his hind end, then lifted his back leg, as to say, "please scratch!"

So I – always obliging to my buddy of 30,700 miles of Cabnet Mountain and vicinity rides – scratcht his back hoove around the caranairy band, and paturn, and fetlock. Ahh, happy horse!

And happy me, too . . . happy to help a friend.

Yesterday, I went to check on ole Rusty. He was napping, which is somewhat uncharacteristic

(them are more editor words. I woulda said "It ain't like him."). So I walkt over, grabed his tail and give it a slite pull. He snorted an lookt at me kind of disgusted, like he was saying,

"WHAT??!!"

I said, "Sorry, Rusty ole pal ole buddy. I was just checkin to see if you still belong above ground!"

He grumbled and laid back down, shakin his head. I'll bet he thins I'm a reel newsance somtimes. Butt I love him anywho!

Well, I better skedaddle. I'm supposed to meet a frind for coffee at Henry's. Stay warm, and keep yer powder dry.

(40 – March 6, 1996) Took my friends out to see Rusty and they brought ther camm corder (video recorder). We got som real good pictures of the kids on ole Rusty, and some of Rustys antiqs of goofing off, with me putting my gloves on his ears, and my hat on his head. Ha!

Soon as the weather gets nice, we is hoping to get shots of the kids riding on ole Rusty. And as I mull threw winters boredom, I hope to write of better rides this summer.

Was seting eating my breakfast after Rose had went to school, when I seed here come a mouse out. It sat in front of the stove, started warming himself. I lookt for Snoopy our cat. There he was, seting outside the front room window, looking in at the mouse! So I got up, but the mouse took off.

I let Snoopy in (he had been watching), I went back and set down, Snoopy went right over to the couch and cought that critter and took it into the dining room for luncheon. He started to play with it.

I said, "Snoopy, kill that thing." Snoopy cought it up again, brought it before me and started to play with it again.

"Snoopy," I said, "Kill that mouse or I will." I grabbed my 44 pistol, cocked it and pointed, ready to finnish the job! But then Snoopy bit it on the scull and CRUNCH! Pop goes the weezel, er in this case, mouse.

"Good job Snoop," I praised him. "Yer a good cat, you did a nicer job than Mr. Smith and Mr.

Weson would of done!"

Some time ago, I ask Rose what she had for lunch at school? She said, "A hamburger, green been, patatos and milk and silverwear, but I did not eat the milk or silverwear!"

Happy trails and be well. Keep yer powder dry!

(41) Reesentlee, WE DUN Roade over to the store that sells things, then decided to go over to grandma's. We did. Then went on down the highway.

Wee found a screen mesh cage sorta thing in the middle of the highway, so me dropt off Rose, then I tried to pick it up with my cane. Rusty jumpt to the side as I bent over to hook it. It didn't work. Maybee I knead a nother hooker.

About thin, here come a motorized car. So off the highway we rode. And then back on. Well, after 3 trys, Rose said, dad, ya want me to git it? Noe, I said, Rusty and I will get it! Well, me tryed one more time, still could not hook it. About that time a nabor come over, and sed, "want me to get that off the highway?"

I said U might as well, sew he did. Rusty's spoiled, and getting older, but he is good most of the time. After all, he has put in more than his time, so, we chatted awile with hour mouths, then went back to grandm'aws.

Eye noticet her wheel barrow, I thought, "I wonder if Rusty would let me use my hooker to pull the handle of it and pull it?" So, I askt Rose to pull it out to where Rusty and I could get at it. I took Rusty over, hookt it up, pulled it around, no problem. Only thing I can figure is Rusty didn't want to be messing around on the highway wen cars were russian buy, besides, the cage of iron was to low for me to retch!

By the way, wile I was talking to the nabor, and was trying to get on Rusty, sombody, reel close fired a shot. Rusty didn't even flinch. That maid up for his screw up on the highway. Well, we got down to the barn and threw my hooker down.

Then sat awile, then talkt to Rusty and Rose a bit, then said Rusty, "lets do the calvery charge!"

Rusty spun around and headed for the gaite. Good enuf! I unadled ant called it a day.

Me'll be looking for you'all when Rusty and me are about town. Youz can recognize me by my brown hooker. Give a waive.

Happy Trails, be well, keep yer powder dry.

(42 – December 21, 1989) One day, one of our days off, my buddy and I went "skinny dipping."

Well he, my buddy, had this fat girl who realy liket my buddy. And this gal, when she out and rented a horse, it was always a pinto horse called "Trigger."

Well, like I said befor me and my buddy grabbed his horse Duke! And I grabbed Drifter, and off to the creek we went. Man it was hot. We got to the creek (a different part of the creek from wher the leach's wher). Anyway, we pealed down to our birthday suits and in we went, AH!

Nice and cool. About 2 hrs. went by, then our horses started whynning. There was a moment of silence, then we heard Trigger's whynnie, and close too. My buddy and I lookt at each other and said, "Beth, the fat broad." She had come out, cought up ole "Trigger" and sneakt to wher she could see through the brush to see all she could see. Well, we jumpt out of that water, hopt on them bare back horses with our bare wet butts, flaping in the breeze we boogeid for the bunk house, and a change of close!

And the fat gal and us just had a good lauph. Oh, what all did she see? She just said, "I'll never tell!" Another day in the life of a cowboy, I guess.

But as I recall, we never seen that fat gal again. I guess it dissapointed her what she saw that one

"hot" day!!

Keep yer powder dry!

(43 – October 25, 1995) Last week I went up to the farm was looking at Rusty and mine's old infiltration course. I couldn't quite remmber how to get their, so I said to Rusty, "you rember our old run up threw ther?"

He lookt up the trail, then lookt down the road towards home, as if to say, "yeah, but, I'm tired, and wanna go home!" So we headed back home. On the way I dropt one rain. Cute! So ole

Rusty stopt and I reacht over with my cain. Uhh! Uhh! There! I got my rain back and we got on our way. It's a good horse that will notice such

61

things and not take off like a bolt. I know of one such horse that would brake into a gallop if you even acted like you werent pain attention.

That horse was a reel trial. He probly got the bullet now.

One day last week after evening feeding, Rusty gave Rose and I our huggys, by my driver he only got one! I was afraid his feeling mite get hurt, so I whisprd to Rusty that he should give the driver another hugy, so's he won't feel left out. Rusty turned and nuzzled the driver on the shoulder, and we all left happy.

I was akst, if horses act like they want to scratch, and ask you to scratch for them, should you?

Well, I scratch Rusty, butt only when we're not riding. If wer'e setting around jawing or if we in the pre-huggy faze, I'll give Rusty a good scratchin' butt only if he asks for it. Otherwise I'm fraid he might get too spoiled. But, if you've got a good horse, a little spoiling won't hurt 'em.

Just my point-of-view. Thanks for asking.

As I was getting ready to feed ole Rusty, he came up and rested his chin on my arm and waited patiently for his supper. I said, "I'm sure glad yer patient, cause I'm perty sllow movin' these days and you'd probly starve if you was in a hurry!"

I always feel so good when Rose goes out and gets Rusty by the main and leads him over to me.

Thers an ongoing message ther it seems. I spect that one day my little Rosebud will have herself a "Rusty" all her own. And if she takes good care, she'll have a good companion most of her life. Sometimes, one good horse is all you ever knead.

On our way down to visit Joyce at the care center, in going by one residence, I seen a horse trailer parkt out front. So today I and Rose stopt and talkt to them folks: three kids and ther mom and grandma. I told them we go see Rose's mom every night! And that my little Rose is 1 of 6 kids we have had raised. The nice lady tolled us that she has a 23 year old quarter horse. I told her that Rusty is 23 and doing perty good.

As we talkt to that fine lady, I notict she too had 6 kids; her yungest is 5, born Aug. 8, her next oldest is 22. Rose is 6 and born on Aug. 3, and our next oldest, Mike is 20. And her horse is 23, she also showed me pictures of her daughter and her poney and of her moms baye quarter horse and uneak pictures of a mountain lion and beaver, too.

That was indeed a fine and pleasnt conversion. Rose and I had to git, so we bid our ados, and that was a good ending to a good day!

This fine lady is not only good looking but a fine horse woman. And though she has not traveled over 38,000 miles in her years of travel on her 23 year old quarter horse – and chaset bear, racet trains, been threw a dynnimite blast, stept in a yellow jack's nests and getting a buzz, and jumping 157 bear, 1 griz, lot of deer and elk, 7 moose enconters as I and Rusty have – I'm sure her daughter has had many great and happy trails and this makes me very happy.

My son Bob and I went on over to the local casieno, put a few quarters in the poker machines. I think I'll stick to the regular 5 card draw and Black Jack, but was a good day for our son Bob.

He won enough to pay for dinner! Then we come home to watch some rodeos on the Country

Satelilte Station.

After the rodeo, we went out to feed ole Rusty. He was mift cause I give him the day off. Rose played with Smokey and Rusty wile Bob moved some hay and played with Rose between her playing with the cat and her teddy bear. Was a good ay. By the who, we also seen our friend

Dan Dunn while we was out.

"Why can't a cowboy make a pitcher of cool aid?" He can't get all that water into that small package.

Wile Rusty was eating his hay, he put his hoov forward and begun scratching his leg, so I reacht out and scratcht it for him. He lookt at me with a kind and loving face, which means, "Thanks, buddy."

Then when I went to walk and lead Rusty over to my stairs to get on, Rusty walkt along side me like a walking crutch, leting me use him to lean on, as if to say, "you scratcht my itch, so I'll help you to the stairs." And he did, cause thats what friends are for.

The other day when we went out to feed Rusty, we drove right on by, headed west! Rusty just lookt, asta say, "Wher ya going?"

When we came back, Rusty started bucking and running around, throwing one hell of hissy fit, as to say, "Get back here and feed me! I do what you want, when ya want, now feed me when I want! Quit fooling around! Darn humans anyway."

We got down to the barn and Bob said," wher ya been? We been waiting for you to get out here and give us a ride!"

Rusty layed back his ears, reared up and said (in his horse talk kind of way), "If you'd quit fooling around on the Hwy we could go byebye!" Then he winneyed.

We got Rusty fed, went on jont, gave some kids a ride then called it a day. Was a happy trail.

Wile feeding ole Rusty, son Bob and Rose played around in the barn. Later Rose and I went on a jont on Rusty up Cedar Creek. Rose racet against Rusty. Rusty, being the gentleman that he is, alloud Rosey to win. What a horse!

We resently had a fine visit with my brother, Jack Bunton, owner of Ram Engine in Spokane, he's a grate guy and a grater mechanic. So if ya have motor trouble, "Ram it" at N. 604 Freya

Spokane, Wash. Ask for Big Bro. Jack H. Bunton, tell 'em Latigo Jim sent ya so ya can get your gas buggy fixt so you can have happy trails for you and yours. Be well, keep yer powder dry.

(44 – August 15, 1991) Wanted to submit a story that got miss placet, that I sent back in "89," anyway, it was when I workt at Harron's Riding Accadamy, S.W. of Havre, it was shortly after I started ther, and just learning about horses, I told my friend, I'm gonna take ole Pinto Pete (a

Shetlen used for kiddy rides only) out side the corral and ride him, my friend said, you better not!

What my friend did not tell me is most horses, especialy used in a corral, that's wher they think they belong and by changing ther thing they get confussed and don't know what ya want!

Well, I was gonna ride Pinto Pete, anyway, so, I hopt on him, bare back, turned him to make him go out, Pete spunn around, headed for the saddle shed, run in, threw the door (wich was open, thank goodness), and dumpt me in between some saddle stalls, and headed for the grain barrle!

Needles to say, I didn't take any of the those shetlan kid's poneys out of the corral for out rides anymore!

Also, was recalling an incident that happened to me at the stockyards.

One sale day, I was pickt to work on the scale (running the cows off the scale), first few hours went well, but then it happened. Scaler yelled 700, and watch it, she's warm. Well I assumed the scale gate opperator opened the gate, well I jumpt in the scale, smackt the critter on the rear, I lookt up, gates closed. I said, "Oh crud, " well words ther similar, anyway that critter turned and came at me, I jumpt back, crosst my arm across in front of my belly, the critter, with horns by the way, came swinging its head, one horn got my arm, and misst my belly, by about an inch, I begun to hit it with my whip, it turned and run out of the scale! By this time the dork operating the gate woke up and opened the gate.

Anyway, I was O.K. A light cut on my arm, scared, and somthing gooshy in my britch's! But, all in all, I was ready for the next critter.

Until next time, Happy Trails and Be Well.

Keep yer powder dry!

(45 – February 1, 1990) As I recall, this feller named Larry bought 5 Arab horses. Amar was

18, and of course well trained and well groomed for the riding! Being a stud and not used fer some time (Amar, not Larry), would make any one leary of just hopping on! Well, Larry come down to my place and askt if I knew anybody that knew how to ride, to check out some horses he'd just bought. I said, Ya, I've rode a little. So we went to wher Amar was kept at the time, **a**nd I cought Amar up, checkt him out, he was fine. The last horse Coa-Coa was good, but ole

Amar made ya fee like a sheik (a real king)! Well, the next up to ride was Saphiera (mare). She give me some static but not bad, all she did was reared up when I first got on. I kickt her again, she come down and took off running and was a good horse after that, she was broke. But just not rode that much. But later kids wher riding her, so she was o.k. The fillies and little colt, wher messt with a little. Moeneac and Rawshaw wher 3 and Shaw (the colt) was about a year or so.

The phillies wher rode off and on, but not hard, not as hard as I rode Amar.

I rode Amar on weekends for about 2 years, 1976 till 1978, the times I rember about ole Amar was trail riding, jumping, old windfalls, running and just plain long walks. Most memrable of times was barrle racing, that old horse love to run the barrles and we got darn good at it too.

Barrles at about regulation length in a stuble, rocky ground with stumps here and ther, we (Amar and I) would go around them barrles in 17 seconds.

One Sunday we went to an Omocksie, ther barrle racers wher doing the barriers in 18-20 seconds. Larry lookt at me and said we should go get ole Amar and realy show em hows it done.

But we did not, didn't want to show up the kids in the Omocksie.

I recall one time after working Amar after he was cool, Larry's Miss's said tie him to that tree and let him graze. I said thats not wise, he will get all tangled up in that long of a rope. She said

No! He won't! It was ther horse, so I tied him to that tree, soon, he was all wrapt and tangled and wrapt to that tree. Since nobody was going to help him I got my knife and climbed in ther with Amar and cut him loose. Amar bolted for home. Then I said, Hey your horse is lose, ya better go get him! That was close, but Amar and I survived!

Keep yer powder dry!

(46) One day, I was out in the yard buildin' a rock garden for the wife, when, I seed this here

Baye horse come down the fence line with all the riggin', but no rider?

I walkt over, cought it up, and said, "Did you lose something?" Turns out that a feller name of

Les was leaving riders who would rent this Baye called Coa-Coa, so I askt Les, if I can ride Coa-

Coa, can I work ther part time? Les said OK, so I took off on ole Coa-Coa, and had no problems. Got the Job!

One day we were headin fer Minor Lake. We got a few miles up Parmenter Cr. Trail someone yelled, "Thers a bear." I thought, oh, oh, rodeo time. Barry Botheman grabbed his 22 pistol and fired a shot in the air and some 200 yards away, out jumpt this little black bear. We scaired him off an' all was well.

Later at the stables, they had this pinto horse, "Plug." When ya got on, it would spin till it throw'd ya. Les, I believ was first. He got on, headed him out, swirl, swirl, cur-plop he went.

Bill got on, swirl, swirl, cur-plop he went. Then was Barry's turn. He got on that Pinto critter, spin, spin, cur-plop he went! I thought oh (expletive deleted), I'm next, so I got on, headed him out, I let out a yell at that not-headed, broomb-tail plug took off in the nicest run ya ever saw. I loved it. I figgered the darn thing got tired of throwing the first 3 riders. But all riders, Les, Bill,

Barry and I never got hurt. But I did hear later, that pinto horse got hit by a car on Kootenai

River Bridge and killed. Rider was O.K.

Next time, "Expierences with Ole Amar, the Arabian!"

Until next time . . . Happy trails, and, do you know how to get a horse out of the bath tub? No?

It's easy, ya just pull out the plug!

Keep yer powder dry!

(47 – April 4, 1991) I'd like to take this time to send a Thank You and Commendation's to who really made "Latigo Jim" possible. First, I'd like to thank Mom and Dad, for without them I would not be here. Love you, Mom.

Next, is my wife Joyce, thanks dear, for everything, yer the best, and especially for putting up with this old horseman or cowboy. Ole bugger anyway. Love you.

Also, Dennis, who taught me a great deal. Thanks pard. My brother Jack, for letting me keep

Rusty on his land for 10 yrs. Rent free.

Harland Geer for all your great help in fencing, roofing and all the rides when I needed them.

Thanks Cedar Creek LoBo.

Also my good friend and compadrae, Larry G. Davis, who has been one of the best of friends.

Thanks, Larry, for the great help and good friendship, and for ole Amarr, the poney chewings, medal roofing, the finest of birthday gifts to me. The 7.65 Arg. Mausar rifle and raising the corner of the kitchen on our home, and well, I could go on. Thanks Larry, God bless . . .

And a special thanks to Don McGrady, who is letting me keep Rusty on his place. Thanks for knowing and understanding horses, and the special kindrin between man and horse, and such.

Thanks Don.

Thanks too, to Ken and Dawn Chase for all your help. And to Dan and Herb of the Cedar Creek

Farm. Thanks very much to Jeri, I didn't forget you. Thanks guys. And last but not least,

Thank God for a fine horse, "Rusty."

And to those I have not mentioned, who helped keep "Latigo Jim" on the trail, keep reading The Montanian. God Bless and be well. I thank you.

Keep yer powder dry.

P.S. Was lookin through the photo albums and come across some photos of when I rode ole Amar Roman style. As I remember, I rode in from Pipe Creek, stopt here at the house, and befor heading back out to Larry's,

I got on ole Amarr and rode him around in the yard, standing on his back (Roman style). Just goes to show you. Great memories never end, especialy of great horses as Amar!

That do 'er fur this week. Until next time, Happy Trails and Be Well.

(48 – March 21 1991) Did you ever run into a black bear with yung? I did, most interesting situation, to be sure. I was coming down an old logging skid road, when I lookt up, here was a black bear on the edge of the road. I got ready to holler at it, it was about 75 yard away, and about the time I was gunna yell "suewie" (Rusty's signal for bear), here come a little black critter running up behind its black bruins mamma! As I and ole Rusty stood ther, she lookt up, then she jumpt towards us. I spun Rusty in an about turn, pulled my pistol, and kickt ole Rusty. We wher runing away from the sow and her cub, I thought anyway, for when I turned to shoot! No bear!

I pulled up, turned, went back to wher she and her kid was, zip! Nothing. She evidently jumpt my way to circle her kid to take up off the hill, when I was thinking she was coming after us. I had the advantage, I was on the retreat, going down hill. Bears cannot run as fast downhill as they can up hill, and I had a gun! And a damn good horse!

The one other time I run into a bear, I should say, one of another 152 bears, was I was coming down from the farm, here by the one mile post was a black bear. It's butt towards me. I wondered how close I could get. So I ambled old Rusty along, then this bear come up on the road, started walking down the road about 50 feet in front of Rusty and at one point, I got within about 10 foot of its behind, then I stopt, let it wonder about 75 ft. I yelled "suewie," it stopt, turned, lookt and snifft the air, then took off up the hill like its tail was on fire. Fun. Yes? Yes!!

But! Dangerous? You bet. But interesting, you gotta admit.

Befor I go, I want to pass along a question I was askt, "Is it O.K. to put oil (such as motor oil) on your horses' hoofs to maintain them?"

No! I would not! I use hoof tar, a hoof tar and neets foot oil mix is good for your poney's feet but I prefer a hoof tar for my horse. Axle greese is good, if ya can find it like it was made a 100 years ago, otherwise it's hoof tar for me! I hope for you and your horses sake, you will do the same. Thank you for asking.

Until next time, Happy Trails and Be Well! And most important! Keep yer powder dry!

(49 – December 11, 1991) Rust and I was going down Cedar Cr. Meadows Road. And saw a big white face cow, she reminded me of a couple of sales at the stock yards, that I have not put down, so hear it is.

One sale, I was on 300 alley, sale was going about normal, till about 4 hrs. into the sale, scaler hollored 700, and watch it, she's hot. That critter come out of thier like a shot, run under the man on the horse, bloking acksess to 300, 100 and 400 alleys. And this cancer eyed, hunk of evil, threw man and horse over an 8 ft. fence into the pen, killing the rider, horse had to be destroyed.

Like I said befor, it's a damn dangerous job! Well, next sale, we wher being pickt for job positions, forman said, Jim, yer on the horse today. Remembering the last sale, I really wasn't to thrilled, but, I went to the saddle stock, pickt a horse, put on an old bucking saddle (you get in one of those and yer going with the horse 90% of the time, and that is as it should be – staying with your horse). Anyway, I went from ther to the tack room, got me a hot shot, went into the sale, things went good, till just about the end. When a hot cow come out, headed for me, I grabbed leather, pointed that hot shot at that ole bit—, cought her on the nose, she spun around and run right down to her pen.

Well, we ended the sale. It went good, a hell of a lot better than the last one.

Then recently, my brother least his place (where Rusty was pastured) to Washington

Construction to dump hiway construction excess (dirt and rock). So Rusty had to move, so we did. But after moving, an opertunity came up to move Rusty to a bigger place with two mares on it. So I put him in for one night, next day, upon leaving, Rusty threw a fit (touch of herd fever), so I moved him back to the first place I moved Rusty. Now he's fine. But while ironing Rusty out I told him, that's a fine way of thanking me, I leave you with two ladies, and then you throw a fit, couse yo don't wanna go to work, so it's back to the corral!

Moral: to muck nukie will make it hard to leave home!

Until next time, Happy Trails and Be Well.

Keep yer powder dry!

(50) After gull blatter surgruy, then treatment for ulcers, I never got Rusty out for a long time till a few days ago. I've been feeling better, sew, I started takin' Rusty out, on the 6th day of taking

Rusty out, we road down two Cedar Cr. flats area, witch we have dun 1,000z of times, well, we turnd off the Hwy. 2, crosst the railroad crossing, went accross, went down a wase down the road turned around, come back to the R.R. crossing, I started Rusty accross, he stumbulled then jurkt, then jurkt again, then I new he had got a hoof stuck inbetween the crossing timber and rail!

Well, I rolled off him. When I did, I ended up under Rusty!

When I sea Rustys belly, and flyin hoofes, I started to roll. I rolled to the edge of the rode.

Lookt up and heres Dave Benifield. He come over, askt if I was alright?!?! I said ya, but Rustys stuck in the crossin. Ol' Dave said he'd call B.N.R.R. and stop any trains, he did. God bless em.

Later I found out Rusty and I held up a train down about Kootenai Springs. But we got something worth more than money on this train hold up! Rusty and I did not get hit ba a train, nore did Rusty and I get hurt bad. Rusty tored up an ankle (his own), cut and bruzed. Me untoucht realy in the crossin. Ol' Dave said he'd call B.N.R.R. and stop any trains, he did. God bless em. Later I found out Rusty and I held up a train down about Kootenai Springs. But we got something worth more than money on this train hold up! Rusty and I did not get hit ba a train, nore did Rusty and I get hurt bad. Rusty tored up an ankle (his own), cut and bruzed. Me un-toucht realy. So God watchs over! Anyway, thanks Dave for all your help for showing up when you did, for helpin Rusty and I back down to Rusty's pasture. And too, thanks Daryl and

Rocky Seaward!

God Bless you all. In conclusion, believe me, I'll never hold up a train again, hope you don't neither, but, accidents do happen!

Also in conclusion, that Feb. 15 ride may be Rusty and I's (mines) last ride. It's time to let yunger riders, and yunger horses, take thier time in the sun. Rusty and I has had hours!

Keep yer powder dry!

(51 – January 12, 1994) Did you ever hunt the ring neckt pheasant? I have, and I enjoy it, but one most memorable moment wile hunting this bird, was when the boss's wife of the riding accadummy askt us to go out and get one, so me, my friend and the boss's son set out. Well we got out in the paschure, lined up single file, and shortly, up flew a ring neckt chinneese bird, my friend who had a 12 GA, fired, misst, bird flew over him, boss's son, who had a 20 GA, pointed and fired, he misst! Bird flew over him. I was last, the bird flew over me, I pulled up my .22, with no back sights, pointed (the gun, that is) and fired, bird went down! Plunk! Well, we pickt up that bird, lookt it over, and not a pellet hole in it, but one .22 bullet threw the side of its head!

Luky? More than lucky, more like a miracle! I could never do that again in a trillion, trillion, quadrillion years! Well, maybe. Anywho, we got a pheasant, tasted good too!

My buddy come up frum back home to go bear huntin, wile we wher huntin bear – that's BEAR as in the family Ursidae in the order of Carnivora, not BARE, as in without clothing – we wher talkin bout a little grey horse of his who was refusing to take a bitt! He said she took the bit fine befour he loaned the horse out, butt the feller he loand the horse to wood stand on the write hand side to putt the bridle on, in trying this the horse fot hymn!

Well win my buddy got his horse back, know weigh yew could git a bridle on the horse, left, or right side, he said, he finely got the bridle on, I first tried the regular whey! T'was a no go, sew he tied up a hind leg of the horse. She fought him again in tryin to get the bit in her mouth.

She went down, he then hogg tyed her, then tried the bridle again, she clammptt her mouth shurt, refusing the bitt, so he stood up, said, "You b—" an kickt her in the teeth. Real lovin sort, he was. Then he tried the bitt again! She took it right off, and he never had any more trouble with getin a bridle on her. In fackt, he said I can wok in her pasture, clap my hands, and here she comes. Good horse, huh?

The lesson here I'd say is, never lend yer horse! Or one of your horses.

Since I dun had to move Rusty and his feet, I mean feed (storage of his winter hay), is in a defferrent place (my folkses' old garage). Win we ride over there, Rusty looks longly at the garage, so after a daze ride I would take him over, open the grage door and give him a small flake o'hay, through it on the ground, then close the garage door. Well, sir, this workt o.k. for awile until one day, Rusty finisht his little flake of hay, then tried opining the garage door with his teeth, I've known horses to open gates and such, but a garage door? Oh well. Horses are not stupid ya know! Shoulda gottim wunna them there garage door openers!

But, ya gotta watch it. I guess. They might become to smart for ther own good huh? Anyways

I've found a good horse will try and please ya, usin his smarts for good things.

Well ole Rusty do er again, after I got threw visiting, wile he (Rusty) was eatin.

I come down to the barn, sat down, started to eat my lunch, Rusty come over, began to nipp and tugg on my coat, as to say, "Git off your duff, let's go." So we do. Er, did.

We road up and down Hwy 2. fer Rustys conditioning, then we headed fer the high country,

Until next time, Happy trails. Keep yer powder dry!

(52 – January 1995) Went out and got Rusty out a little the other day. Went and did our normal everyday routine stuff witch we enjoy, that is, get gramas mail an check other places out. Butt today we did something differnt. I took Rusty round a telephone pole, and a stump and a old satilite dish pole (dish was gone).

After that, we headed back to the barn. Befor unsaddling I pulld some snow off the barn roof an some of it droppt on Rusty's head. "Oops," says I. "Great fun, a Rusty?" I said to Rusty. Well,

I thought so anywhey.

A friend of mines girl frind come with us to feed Rusty one evenin. She said she has a BLM horse mustang, and would really like to see Rusty.

I said sure. Upon seein Rusty I showed her what he looks like when he mimicks Bullwinkle the moose. I put won of my gloves over each of his ears.

Nexst, I said, "Here's how confident and gentle ole Rusty is," as I pealed back his I lids, run my fingers up his nose an in his ears. She (my friends girlfriend) liket that so much she kisst Rusty on the fourhead. Well, I just patt Rusty on the neck or get huggys! Shure is cool. As them critters do for us, we should do for them!

My yungest son ask me watt was the crazyest thing I ever dun? After I thunk about it, I said,

"First thing was jumpin and fallin off runnin horses doing stunts. Next was workin at a stockyards and runnin through about 2 foot of cow crap and such (you gotta be crazy to njoy that). Nexst was going threw a dynnimite blassed with ole Rusty).

But buy far the crazyest was chasing a bear up a mountain side. An I guess right up ther with that is when Rusty reard over backword and fell on me in 1979.

Going threw forest fires and encounters with 8 mooses was knot to crazy. Or meeting a grizz bear iether.

Oncet when I rowed cocoa horse threw the Lager Days parade, somebody threw a couple of fire crackers under him, but that didn't get to crazy. Then ther was the time old amarr the stud horse fell with me in the Logger Days parade. And, oh ya, almost forgot when ole amarr and I run in

Timberline Auto's garage, made a circle and come out again. That was perty crazy and funky.

An finaly ole Rusty and I getting caught in a R.R. crossing "holding up a train!" That was crazy.

Fie think of any other I'll write of it later.

Got Rusty out again the other day an went kyote hunting a little, then went down to gramma

Junes. Wile ther I thought I'd wipe off her satilite dish with my hands. Well, as I was brushin the snow with my hand Rusty started to brush with his lips. I said, "Atta a boy, team work!"

Ah, I should tell the beginning of our story. When I got out ther to feed Rusty, I found the gate froze shut. Wile trying to get it open, Rusty was running around, finally, he stopt lookt at me questioningly. I said, "The gates froze. Can't get in?!?!" He shook his head, and reard up. I said,

"Keep yer shirt on. I'm comin." Sew I crauwld under the fents, went and fed the old boy.

Ah, now to saddle up and get on. Rusty refussed to stand still. Second time I tryed he still would not, so I said, "Stan'd still or I'll bop ya!" I tryd again, he moved again, so I boppt him between the ears. He stood still for me then.

Now to get out threw a froze gate! Furst I pulld with my caine. No good. Bout that time, a friend come by and releast Rusty from the pasture. Thanks again Toni. Then we went kyote hunting and etc. Mostly etc.

A perty good day, could of done without the rain, though! Oh well, got most chores done!

Didn't get know kyotes. "Another day tommarrow" or sum such frays.

I forgot to tell ya, come time to go home (Rusty's place), he did not want to come home! See what a bop on the head will dew! Ya get team work and they don't wanta go home!

Happy trails and be well, keep yer powder dry!

(53 – March 1995) Was remberin a few years ago when I use to ride from Cedar Creek, up around Plumber Hill, and come out to what yewstabee known as Dutches Food. Well, I come up our reglar sckid road. Bout 2 miles from CD Creek, "Bingo," hears a little cinnomin bear! I yelled, it took off!

Next day, about the same time a day, here comes Rusty and me, bingo again! Here's the same little cinnomon bear! I got my gun ready, yelled and the bear tuk off! This time the bear was about 500 yards from wher I jumpt it the day befor.

Next day, here comes ole Rusty and me, about the same place, "Shazam!" another bingo! But this time, the bear was about a mile from wher we jumpt it. I and Rusty got ready . . . I yelled, the bear took off. After that,

I made several trips threw ther on my way to town and I never seen that cinnom bear again.

It was a good bear, never caused us trouble, and it always steerd cleer of peephole. But jumping it three times in a row was kinda weird!

But not seeing it after the third time I figured it musta got tired of me and Rusty walking through his plate, so decided to move to better eatins. Witch was o.k. with me and Rusty.

My pardner, Robert Anderson Jr., and I have been travailing back and forth on Hwy. 2 west, and the other day we notict that the west end of the four lane has pot holes that are realy getting bad!

Fact is, I'm afraid to ride Rusty down threw ther. If we fell in one it would probly take a weak to find us! But sereously, ther getting perty bad. Ifn you don't believe me, ask Robert and his car,

Dodge Aspen. Every time we hit one, that Dodge says, "Ouch!"

Hope the Hwy. Dept. will fix it as soon as possible.

Feedn Rusty the other day, I was waiting for him to clean his plate. I set doodleing, or reading the paper, or whatever. Well this time old Smokey the barn cat jumpt up in my lapp and sat, and as Rusty grazed towards me, he got close enoulph so ole Smokey started sticking his nose in

Rusty's ear. Rusty would shake his head and Smokey again would stick his nose in Rusty's ear.

Stick, shake, stik, shake.

I put Smokey down and said, "Enoulf of you getting your nose out of place." Rusty was greatful for my intervention on his behalf.

After victuals we rode up Cedar Creek an checkt an old deer carkus for kyotes. Nun in site.

We called it a day, so we headed back to the barn and pasture. But bfore we left I sat on Rusty turned sideways for awile. I rubbed and petted him fer a bit becoz we're "buds!"

Then I got off, unsaddled, and went down to Henry's for coffee and B.S. Was a good day.

Yer probly wondering bout horse conditioning? What Rusty and I use to do is take an old deer trail up Plumber Hill, a winding trail, with holes and wind falls (widow makers). The trail went for about 3,000 yards (9,000 feet, 1.704 miles, etc.) but the steepest and rouffest part was only about 200 yards. The rest was farely level butt narrow with wholes in the trail.

Ole Rusty and I would trot the easier trail, then run up the ruffer 200 yard part. Sinteresting how most horses are sew careful with the placement of ther feet, and judgment of jumpts and jumping other obsticles. And Rusty's just as good as the best of 'em.

After getting up on a loggin rode we go downhill from there. After about half mile (2,640 feet,

880 yards, etc.) thers a bogg about 20 feat long, 8 or 10 ft. wide, take that at a walk or trot. From ther it's a leisurly walk to Libby, about 7 miles.

This is a good ride, especialty for a yung green broke horse or mule. Main thing is, if you have a horse or mule, ride 'em! Not only for excersize, but for companionship!

Guy goes to the doctor. Doc says, "Ya got three days to live. How you gonna spend them?" He says, "I'll spend them with my mother-in-law. It will be the longest 3 days of my life!"

Thnext day, Rusty and I went out an checkt Grandmas, then gave a 2 year old little boy a ride on

Big Red, then visit with his mom. Found out she was borned the same day as me. Well, almost.

Her birthday was in 1976, mines was in 1944.

She askt, "How old are you?" When I told her, she said, "You don't look that old." I coulda hopt off ole Rusty and kisst that little lady! She really made my day! Great gal! With a great son. Well, I put up ole Rusty and headed back home.

Happy trails and be well. Keep yer powder dry!

(54 – April 1994) Today was another speshull day for Rusty and me. Apon retruning from

C.C.F. I stopt to pickup mom's mail, well Rusty decided to do the same I guess, for when I leaned over to reach in the mail box for mom's mail, I noticet ole Rusty had opened the 4th mail box down, and was looking in it, I said, "Rusty, that is none of our bussness, so get out of ther!"

He straitened up his head, I closed the mail box and delivered mom's mail. "Poney Express," well, we got back to Rusty's place, and after I put him up, while Rusty was eating, a stray cat that was hanging around, umpt on Rusty's back, and doug in its claus, Rusty just stood ther, looking back at the cat and me, I grabbed the cat, swated it on the butt, and dropt it on the ground and said, "Have some respect for your better's, cat! This time it was a swat, next time it will be a bullet!"

Started out for the farm, typacle day, sorta, as we got about a mile and a half from the place,

Rusty threw up his head, then lookt to the side, "O.K. son," I said, "Bear Huh!" Let's go get em . . . got my gun out, we whent about another half mile, and here on the road, fresh, I mean, real fresh bear dung! Well, we never seen no bear, but its neet how big ole red horse watchs over ole

Jim. Ah, with the Good Lord's help of course!

Was setting in the corral wunts remembering the horses that came and gone, with Rusty standing by me, I was telling him. Rember the little colt we had in here Rusty? What a little dweeb, eh, cute as a button, and aunry as hell, but a horse! I also rember what fun the little teard had when its owner brought an old plastic milk jug with some small pebbles in it, and threw it to the colt.

What a ball that little teard was having tossing and kicking that milk jug. So much fun in fact,

Rusty had to have one, so I made one for him, then we had two colts, well one colt, and one guilding who thought he was a colt.

Both having fun anyway, until Rusty had to go to work.

This winter was most interesting! First no snow, then about 2 foot in the valley here in and around Libby, MT, but Rusty and I ride anyway! Since my legs don't work so good no more, I have a hard time wading through the deep snow, so come time for Rusty and I to go, I climb upon the manger, step on Rusty, out the gate we go, ride on down the folks garage, saddle up, and off for a day's riding we go!

Befor, and the over 31,000 miles I've rode Rusty, and the cancer and radiation I had in 1972, it's a wonder I'm still walking at all!

But, the Lord provides. And with a horse like Rusty, he is great medicine! Until next time, happy trails and be well. Keep yer powder dry!

(55 – May 18, 1994) The other day I seen a feller whom I have not seen for quite a spell, he said, "Man, you've had that horse for a long time! You are gonna have to get another!"

I said, "Nope! Rusty's my last horse! I'm getting to stowed up any anymore, so after Rusty, ther will be no more other for me!!"

For when your legs don't work, and your horse is going blind, your days are numbered, but we have road the wind and have memories of gold, and isn't that what life is all about? For over 12 years, and covering over 32,000 miles of most interesting, but happy, trails is good!

And did you know! That the only time a horse has all for feet on the ground is when they (it) are

(is) standing! At any gate, they only have no more than 2 feet on the ground at one given time.

Interesting, and most gracious and uneak you must admit!

I member once when Joyce and I was out to McGrady's wile visiting with Don. Rose, our youngest, doughter, who was 3 at the thyme, took off for the barn, so I walkt on down, when I got ther, Rose was in the coral with Rusty, I called Rose, then told her to come out of the corral!

She didn't, then I called again, this time with a firmer voice, getting madder! She still refused to exit the corral. So Rusty layed his ears back, shook his head, jumpt a little, spookt Rose perty good, here she come running to dad and gladly!

I thankt Rusty for sending Rose out to me, and making her mine dad. As all baby siters should make kids mind, huh?

In talking to my boy bout hunting, fishing, the woods and stuff, as we walkt, we wher talking about the river. I said, do you know wher Quarts Creek emptys into the river? Kootenai River?

He said yes, well I said, right accross the river, ther, I took Rusty into the river, back in 19 and 81

I guess it was to see if Rusty new how to swim and he does swim real good! Water was up to

Rusty's jaws, and up and around my shoulders, and, "but dad," my son said, you do not know how to swim! I said, not a stroke, or yes, I can swim like a rock! But was interesting. The chalenge and everything turned out well! But, agian, I urge you not to try this, even if you know how to swim the Kootenai is a vicious river, Rusty and I just walkt out, dropt in a hole, then Rusty swam back to the river bank, but I found out what I wanted to know! Rusty can swim! But I'll never do it again.

I was askt, my horse is on pasture and chews on the fents, why is this?

Again, befor I ansure this, let me say, I'm no expert horseman, but I would say he's one of 3 things!

1. Needs salt

2. Or lacking a certain mineral in its system (diet)

3. Just plain bored

So if you do not have a "horse block," I suggest you get one. I keep one iodized salt block and a horse block wher Rusty can get to em any time, plus I ride, quite a bit.

Anyway, this schould solve your problem, if not, I'd do two things!

Consult a veternarium and write to esquirine magazines. They have encountured this same problem and may have a different solution.

But good food, salt, water and excersize works for Rusty and me! Thanks for askin, and I hope I helpt you and yer horse.

Was recalling when a friend (same fellow who owned "Dizzy" and was the same fellow with whom I had a snow ball fight), well, anyway back about 1980, we rode about all day and then after going with my friend up to his place Rusty and I headed for Cedar Creek. By the time we got to Plumber Hill, it was dark, real dark, well we kept on hooving it, alonge Hwy. 2 and if you are familiar with the Hwy. 2 befor they widend it, you will rember thers very little room to be walking, especially walking a horse along! Well, cars and rigs would go by, headlights on bright **a**nd would pass with in 8-12 inches from us and Rusty would not as much as twitch an ear, or hair, when them gas buggies would go buy! We have went along the Hwy durring the day many, many, many times and done super fine!

Wich proved one more time, I believe God must of broke the mold when ole Rusty foaled!

Wee celebrate hunting heritage and culture during the week of Sept. 15th threw Sept. 21st please show your support of our hunting and heritage culter during this weak. Wear your pro-gun, or hunting organization gear, or display the American flag.

And for those who will be out hunting please display the American flag lets see your support for

Montana's most precious sport. Hunting not only benefits Montana economically, but provides meat for one's table and helps keep and preserrve game animals species. And finaly, hunting teachs ruggedness and responsability.

I thank you.

Keep yer powder dry.

(56) Before I git to the "snowball fight on horseback" and Rusty tiff with a grey trick horse, I want to tell of my friends black horse called "Dizzy," and boy she lived up to that, she was broke to pack I guess but not riding. Well, I remember my friend and a farrier coming out to shoe

"Dizzy," we had that horse hogged tied, laying on the arena floor, and she would still fight, I recall sitting on "Dizzy's" neck, my friend on its head, then Dizzy would explode off my friend and I would go; but after sacking "Dizzy" out, and repeated sitting on her face, we got her shoed.

Later she became a pretey good saddle horse. I was pretey proud of my friend fer sticking with it, if it was my horse, it would have been dog food by now, or should I say then.

Happy trails. Keep yer powder dry!

(57 – Pony Tales) About 3 years ago I met these folks, all of who were riding horses, as well as I

(Rusty, of course). Anyway 2 were 3 year olds, with riders of not much more experience, and 2 with experienced riders and broke horses.

Well this fellow says to me, "This has been quite a day." I said, "Oh yeah!" He said, "Yeah, we seen a couple of deer, an elk. Then he said, "By golly, there's a bear." Well this I figured: there's two solutions. Ignore it and hope the green broke horses won't throw their riders; or pull my pistol and fire some shots. But then we will for sure need an ambulance.

So I did what every good stump jumper should do. When in doubt, charge! So we did . Run that little blacky up in the toolies.

Got back; one fellow said, "You can not do that. Horses don't like bear."

"Well," I said, "What did you see?"

The fellow said, "What would you have done if the bear would have turned on you?"

"Simple," I said. "I'd a killed it. But you see, black bears are 98% feared of humans and will almost always run, and since it had no young and was not cornered, I gambled on it running. I was right." And it was fine a day and a fine ride.

(58) I was recallating once when I noticet a bunch of horses, 10 or so, over at the nabor's. When

I saw the nabor, I askt, "What's up?"

He said his relatives was heare to go big game huntin. Well my friened, only about 2 days later, all his kin was gone! I saw him later during huntin season and askt, "Wheared they go so quick?

What happened?"

He said, "We tuk about 500 pounds of pellets up to Hornets Ridge, but the horses got so tired and sweaty, they decided to quit and go home."

"Whers home?" I inquisited.

"Wisconson."

Then I askt, "What sit like there?"

He said it was flat country like the east side of Montana. Turns out their horses wasn't accustomated to our steep countryside. They got tuckered!

Personnaly, I think they should have stayed here a few daze and give their horses time to adjust to the altatude. They spent all that money for a two-day huntin trip in Montana! Next time they decide to throw money away, I hope they throw sum of it my way! I could sure use it.

May I suggest: Give your horse time when going to another state to adjust to altitudes or atmisfier. They will handle a lot better.

I was resently askt what clouthing I wear on the many rides I've been on?

Itsa question I never expected! But I wear in the summer Wrangler genes, Acne boots with combination riding and walking heel and a vieriety of long slieve shirts, plus a smart cap or hat, pending on the wheather.

Wintertime I wear longjohns, a pear of blue jeans and 2 shirts, a jacket and a long saddle coat. In

Montana ya dress in layers or ya frieze, don't ya know! When I ride in brushy places I wear my canvas pants.

My winter attire also includes a natty pair of winter boots that fit the stirrups on my saddle. Oh, most portant: My six shooter. I got that with me winter or summer.

Rusty? He just wears his birthday suit . . . plus my saddle and bridal.

And speakin of clouths, I wish to pass on a story I heard from grandma June.

The women of the house told the buttler she was going out for awile. When she come back, she saw the butler and got flusturd. She ordered him to follow her into her "boodwaur," then she told him, "Take off my blouse!" So he did.

"Now take off my bra!" He did.

"Now take off my skirt!" So he did.

"Now take off my panties!" So he did.

Then she says, "This is the lass time I'm gonna tell you: QUIT WEARING MY CLOUTHS!"

I heard someone say "Latigo" wrong the other day, so I figgered I oughta rite the correct pronouncitation. Its pernouncet "LAT'-i-go." Sents I aint got International Phonetech Alphebat cymbals, I'll use some reglar, Old West pronoucer tips: First sylabull, LAT, rimes with CAT.

Second sylabull is a short "i" like in "insipid." Third is "go." Rhymes with "go."

"Latigo" is a Spanish word for strap or belt. It's the strap that holds yer horses saddle in place.

It goes under his belly.

The other day, after duing our chores of checking on grandma and getting her male, I spotted an abandoned vehicle, so Rusty and I went and lookt it over. Wernt musch to see, thuough. Just another Lincoln County rodeside attraction.

Went to Kalispell the other day, just for a daze drive. The day was going good until on the way back we was overpast by a logg truck carrying its trailer piggy back style.

When the truck got about 20 carlinks ahead of us, the trailer fell off part way, throwin sparks all over! Reglar fireworks display! My boy slowed down and I got on the C.B. radio and hollord at the fellow. He, the log truck driver, pulled off the road and took care of the problem.

Everything was ok ther so we bookied on down the road. Then at about mile post 60 a deer came out on the Hwy. and "Smook!" We gott him! American car versis American deer. Deer lost! We stoppt and got out to put him out of mysery. I grabbed my pistol to finish him and woe! Here was in two pieces!

So I saved myself 90 cents ther on a bullet. All in all was a great day! Cept for the deer!

Coarse, the trailer coulda falled off the truck and piled onto us. Butt it din't, thank you Lord.

And that deer could of flipt up and come threw the windshield, or threwed us in the ditch, but didt.

Thank you Lord! The only damage done was a knockt out head light and signal light. Nobody got hurt. Cept the deer.

Thank God.

Happy trails and be well. Keep yer powder dry!

(59 – March 9, 1994) Was remembering a time I road over to the now-defunkt Montana City

Old Town. I rode into town, hear come a nabor's dogg German Shepard. On the charge, I askt

Alberto, is this your mutt? He said no, run him off wood you? I said sure! I weeled Rusty around, yelld, "Gitt!" Rusty took off, we run that "Dirty dog clean out of town!" Sorta speak.

The dog sure left in a hurry and never did come back. And from then on we had a good day visiting with the tourist.

The other incident I wish to right of was when I was coming back from old town, I stopt by

K.C.L.B. The feller come out, we chatted a bit, then he said, "Why don't you ride on in." Then he opend the door, I started Rusty up the steps, towards the door. He (the fellow from K.B.L.C.) shut the door and yelled, "No, no! I was just kidding!" So I stopt and said good buy and left.

No, right.

Then won other time, this gall come ridin' her horse up to me, said, "A dog down ther run out and bit her horse." I said, "Oh, ya, show me." Sew we went down larch street, low and beholed here come a black lab (dog, not laboratory), the gall stopt her horse, I went after the lab, as the dog went to run away. Rusty kickt him in the butt. Run him right up to his door! Then I left.

Dog never chaste horses anymore iether. Well, none I heard of. Well, until next time . . .

Happy trails and be well! Keep yer powder dry!

(60) Took ole Rusty out the other day, we headed for Libby, got about a mile and half from

Cedar Cr. and since Rusty has not been out that much this winter, I figured he was getting tired, so I turned him around and headed back for Cedar Creek, when he stopt! I said you want to go on to town? Rusty lookt back towards Libby, as to say, "Ya, I don't want to go home yet!" So I said, "O.K. Let's go to Libby!" On the way I said, "Well we'll ride on down to the feed store, and get you a treat." Well, we got to the store, no owners so dissapointedly, we headed back for

Cedar Creek, and on the way back I told Rusty, well, when we pick up grandma's mail, I know she will have a treat, we got to Cedar Creek, checkt the mail, "No mail!" Well I said, "Lets go to grandma's anyway." So, upon arriving ther grandma was gone! So, I said, "Rusty! We have put in a full day! I know we have a treat for you back at the barn!" Well we called it a day! A perty good day and quit. Wher upon Rusty finally got a treat! But his first treat was just geting out on the trail with Latigo Jim.

The other day friends of mine come out to pick me up, when they got ther my friend's Mrs. and ther daughter stood on one side of Rusty, whos loose and nibbling on some hey. Anyway, I began to tease my friend's Mrs., when I got the best of her, she told her daughter to go over and hit Jim (me), so the little gal walkt around Rusty and slapt my arm, after she did, Rusty layed his ears back at the 10 yr. old girl, as to say, "Hey, you don't hit the boss!" I said, "It's alright

Rusty, she's just playing." Rusty went back to eating. Until next time.

Hey, my horse is lose! That was Rusty, back on April 17, 1990.

What happened was, my friend come out to get some old metal roofing at the pasture and left a gate open, wich is easy todo, because even I have trouble keeping track of the 9 gates at the place, but ole Rusty stayed ther! Lose all night and never took off, neet eh! Yes . . . and since

Rusty is a proud cut guilding, I had to jive Rusty a bit, I told him, "Boy yer not very smart, or yer just geting old, hear's your chance to be lose and take off, and you didn't, you didn't even take off and go visit that cute mare across the way! Tsk, tsk . . ."

After a coupla years of care taking Cd Cr. Farm I figured since I and ole Rusty was on our own, for undesirables, I'd have an "ace in the whole," ya might say, and that was, I tought Rusty to strike with a front foot, dissebleing or cursching a man's chest, upon my signal! And until this date, fortunaley, we never had to use superior force in any manor, but we always tried to be ready!

Happy trails and be well. Keep yer powder dry!

(61 – July 1994) During the Hwy. 2 construction between Libby and Troy, MT they had set up what they called "windows," it was a two hr wait wile they workt up ahead on the Hwy. Well, wile folks wher waiting, I and ole Rusty would go up and down the line, visitin with some folks.

Won time, I was talkin to a couple of guys, subject guns and hunting and well, after awile a couple, a man and wife came by, stopt, the Mr. said, "Boy if you was in Canada, wher we are from, you could not do that," referring to me standing ther with my sixshooter on my hipp. And that it is illegal for a citizen to own a handgun or carry one in Canada. I said, "Ya, I know that's why I live down here!" The Canadian then said, "Well our crime rate is lower!" I then said,

"Whoa, wait a minute, your wrong ther sir. By your statement, your saying gun control is the ansure to Americans crime problem? Gun control and/ or gun bans?" He said, "Yes." "Well sir," I said, "lets look at that. A few years ago, Kennisaw, GA passt a firearms maintence law, you have to own a gun, unless egzempted because you hate them, or are scared of guns. Wel, at about the same time a town in Illanois passt a law, totaly banning handguns, and stricly regulatin long guns, crime in that city went up, and is increasin!"

Wher in Kenasaw, GA, ther is vertualy no crime at all! "Now sir," I queried, "What does that tell you?" (Both city's are about the same in population size.) He said, "That does not say anthin." I said, "It don't?" I said then what about Wash. D.C.?!? It has the strictest gun laws in the U.S. and also has one of the highest crime rates in the U.S.! Hmmmm, then the fellow I was talking to said, "Well they should ban semi-automatic rifles and pistols. I said, "They should?

Why?" Well he said, "Look at what Purdy did in a school yard in California!" Yes I said lets look at that, first Purdy shot them kids with an AK-47, that is a fully automatic rifle, a machine gun, witch are realy regulated in the U.S. And the shootin was tradgic. But, Purdy was drivin a

Ford pick-up witch he parkt backa the school building, now I believe Purdy killed three kids and wounded 15 with that Ak-47, but had he done drove threw that school yard with that Ford pickup, for sure he would have killed 25 top 50 kids and woundin at least a hunnert more! If so, would you stand up and cry for the outlawin of all Ford pick-ups?? But at any rate, now in

California, all semi-automatics are band in the state of California! And ther crime rate is goin up! Just befor the window opened, I said, If you favor any kind of gun control, or bans, in the name of fightin crim, you had better outlaw rocks, trees, table knifes, razors, sizzors, etc. It is

B.S. people kill people and people wher killed long befor guns was invented! As they wher walkin away to get in their cars, I askt, only honest citizens obey the law, why do you support penalizing us?? In conclusion, it is a proven fact that guns, even semi-autos, in the hands of citizenry, are a crime prevention. Itsa fact. And proven.

Legislation against an inatimate object is not the ansure. But education of firearms and such are, is, am! For I have not found anybody who can ansure my question and that is: How many guns, layin their, fully loaded, has killed or injured anyone? But I know the asnure, "Nun!" It takes some idiot or crazy to do evil with it, as they would any weopon, so why deprive the honest citizen of protectin his family, his self, his property, his nabor?? His country?

Restore and protect your right to own and bear arms. Keep yer guns! An keep yer powder dry!

Yours for an armed citizenry.

P.S. Happy trails and be well!

(62 – April 1993) Winter time reminds me of horse back riding in winters past, in remembering,

I recaled an accident I had with Rusty, I thought I'd make the 7 mile trip around plumber Hill, one winter several years ago. Well I found we could not make it up our usal summer trail, so I

Zig-Zagged up the Hill, til we got to the old scid road, upon reaching it I found the only way to get on the road was to get off, walk down a little slope, then get back on ole Rusty and boogie down the road. Well, sounded simple enoulph, well, I got off, stept down the little slope, swipbang, down I went, and when I was flat on my back, I lookt up, here's Rusty looking down at me, as if to say, "What you doing down there?" I could not help but lauph. Anyway, I regained my composier. Well, I collected myself together, and got on and the rest of the day went well.

In recalling this, reminded me of the following summer my boy wanted me to take him with me, so I said o.k . . . . well, we headed up one of them summer time trails, on the 7 mile treck around

Plumber Hill and we come to a perty steep slope, so I told Bob, my son, when we go up the slope, lean forward, he said o.k., so I kickt Rusty, he started up the slope, Rusty lopet up to the top, Rusty flattend out I tried to straiten up, but Bob was still leaning forward. I said, "Bob, set up!" All he did was say, "Ah, ah," so I lookt behind at Bob, here he is, all drapet over Rusty's butt, legs dangleing. I stopt Rusty. Got him straitened out, and finish our ride, but Bob never rode with me again. Spookt him I guess . . .

Well, he got over it, but just don't care for them 2 seated horses!

Was remembering when I had my cowboy hat cleaned and reblockt, the next day, I saddled up ole Rusty and headed up to Cedar Lakes, on the way back it started raining, I could feel the rain coming through the seem around the head ban, well I thought, last time I'll have my hat cleaned.

Well, here come some folks a man, his wife and ther first kid, well they took a look at me, I said hi, they returned the greeting, then I said, going to the lakes? They said yes, and askt how much further are the lakes? I said, about another 2 miles, they thankt me and went on, all the time though, they kept looking at me real funny. I shruged it off, got back home, went into the house, went into the bathroom to wash my hands, and lookt in the mirror, here's red streaks of red dye from my hat when it was leaking, ah huh, now I know why them folks lookt and acted so funny!

When I met em, I must of scared them folks perty good, wich I felt bad about but that's the way she goes some time. I gotta admit, I didn't look too good.

Upon ending a days ride, chores, I put Rusty up, I gave Rusty a huggy, and he gave me one in return, and another one, and another one and he realy didn't want me to leave but what a horse eh! So I left, whent to turn on the water, Rusty started to realy whynnie, I stopt, told him, "Keep your shirt on, I'm turning on your water." He quieted, I turned on the water, came back, talk to him, til the window opened, to go back into Libby.

We talkt of trails well traveled, tracks in the snow, that are no more . . .

The prarie's wide, mountains devine, and now we, Rusty and I, too, will soon be gone!

Until next time, I hope . . .

Happy trails and be well. Keep yer powder dry!

(63) Befor I tell of more happenings with Rusty and I, I wanted to tell of a time that happened at the stockyards with my brother and I. One sale I was put on 300 alley, my brother Jerry was put on 400 alley, sale was going perty good, til the scale operator hollard 705, and watch it, she's hot! And boy was she, she come out hot on the prod! She come out, hit the horse, knock them down, she come down towards 300 alley, I swung my cross gate, cot her right in the hinde quarters, but a few hopps she got by and headed for 400 alley! I lookt down towards my brother and ther's Jerry, standin on the ground readin a book, I yelled, and yelled, he didn't hear me, did you ever try to yell over 100's of balling maingy cows? It's hard.

Well, seconds after my last hollar at Jerry, for some reason Jerry turned, lookt thrugh the corner of the fence, seen that mad, cancer eyed, critter comin, Jerry dropt the book, skampered up the fence, I never seen him move so fast, I was never so scared, I thought sure he'd bought the farm!

But he was o.k. and another day's work at the job. At the stockyards.

I meant to put this in with an earlier colum but it got misst placet.

Went out to feed Rusty, Nov. 15, guess it was, and here's Rusty lamed up, front left foot, upon checkn it, I thought it was a tendin, so doctored that, then figured I should have Rusty's shoes pulled, so called my shoer and friend Mark, he came right out and he was checkin Rusty's front left hoove, before pulling the shoe, he found Rusty had poket a hole threw his hoove, he lancet it, put some medicine in it, and Rusty felt a lot better! Then Rusty came up to Mark and give him a huggy!

Rusty's doing a lot better now . . .

Good friends and good horses if you have these, yer very fortunate . . .

Read all the signitures in The Montanian wanting my calum, "On The Trail With Latigo Jim" every 2 weeks! Was great and heart warmin to see this . . .

Thank you, and too, I hope to see you all as often as I can in The Montanian.

God bless, and take care, and be well . . .

Happy trails and keep yer powder dry!

(64 – March 31, 1993) Was out setting with Rusty other day (witch is far inbetween for ole

Rusty and I's getting together anymore). Anyway, wile workin on some of my saddle tack,

Rusty goes an stands on the other side of the barn, so I said, that's cool, Rusty . . . I don't get out hear to spend much time with ya, then when I do, ya stand on the other side of the barn! So, wile

I could see him threw a crack in the barn wall, I hallard, "RUSTY! RUSTY!" He threw up his head second time I called, here he come to the door, lookt in at me, like as if to say, Here I am, you o.k.?

I guess my tune of voice made him think I needed help, so here he come! And after all, isn't that what friends are fore?

Oh, a friend an I sat down an figgered out Rusty and I's milage from Aug. of 1978 to about Aug. of 1992. It was 38,410 miles, took awile, since Rusty aint got no mileage meter! But if you seen his shoes, you would see the miles! But I see the memories!

Oh, by the by, I done put them miles on Rusty without an oil change. Had to tune him up once in awile. But all and all, great miles and great times!

Smatter of fact, I was recaling a time when I went up to the place, folks who own the place wher cutting down a couple trees for an arch way for the entry to the farm.

Well, when Rusty an I rode up, they'd just cut one. So's I said, could I an ole Rusty pull that one out for you? They said ya! An so we did. Got Cedar Creek Farm off to an old fashion start. An that archway still stands today. As all good things should.

Diju ever ride your poney down the hwy? You proble have, but have you rode em down the

Hwy. at night? I have, and have autos come by an have gravl sprayed against your mount, and only have em flinch a little? Ole Rusty has!

An have you have them Big 18 wheelers go by you, bout 6 inch's from you an your horse and not even so much as have your mount flintch? Ole Rusty don't even twitch! If your horse is as

Rusty, you not only have a well broke poney, but a good friend!

Until next time, happy trails and be well. Keep yer powder dry!

(65 – July 1, 1992) Since Rusty and I don't git out mutch, I catch him up, on days we don't ride, an we have watt I like to call, Carrot Hour, he eats some carrots and hay, I eat on a sandwich and cooke's an sip on a jug of apple juice or cranberry. Well, wee do this for about 3 or 4 ours, then

I generaly do some choir's, then, feed ole Rusty his supper and call it a day.

One day not long ago, after our Carrot Hour, I put Rusty up, went an did some fencing (cedartype, not yer thrust an parry-type). Then fed Rusty his supper, then I went an checkt that I had everything pict up an gate's closed. Everything was A-o.k., it was, well, I walkt aroun, went to go out a gait by the barn, Rusty had walkt up behind me, grabbd my coat with his teeth, an pulled me back. He did this 3 times, as each time I would reach fer the lock on the gate, as if to say, don't leave, stay, so I turnd, told him, "It's o.k. I'll be back shortly." He turnd, and went back to finishin his hey.

When you have a horse for a frind, you have somthing speshal. Until next time, happy trails and be well. Keep yer powder dry!

LATIGO JIMS ECONOMIC HORSE CARE

It is my hope to prevent horse abuse and neglect, all you need

To give T.L.C. work labor of love.

1. Bonding is commitment.
2. Good horse care means love and dedication.
3. Keep it simple crawl in their hearts and minds, their heads and confidence in following you. Love continued always.
4. Be patient, persistent and repetitious.
5. Keep your horse as close to their natural environment as possible.
6. Horses first aid kit at least a pair of 'Easy Boots', small can of bag balm, extra hoof pick, small bottle of peroxide, small belt, gauze and a pocket knife.
7. Did you know horses eyes can see at night like you and I on a cloudy day? Also they are blind 4 inches to 6 inches from their face?
8. Whiskers on their nose are there to sense what kind of person you are.
9. Watch the treats, such as black licorice, mints, granola bars, and carrots, no apples,
10. These things that I've mentioned got Rusty through over 38,400 miles and them some. My faithful Rusty lived 32 human years, I had him from 1978 - 2003. He passed in his sleep a fine horse and a blessing.

"Happy Trails and Keep Your Powder Dry.

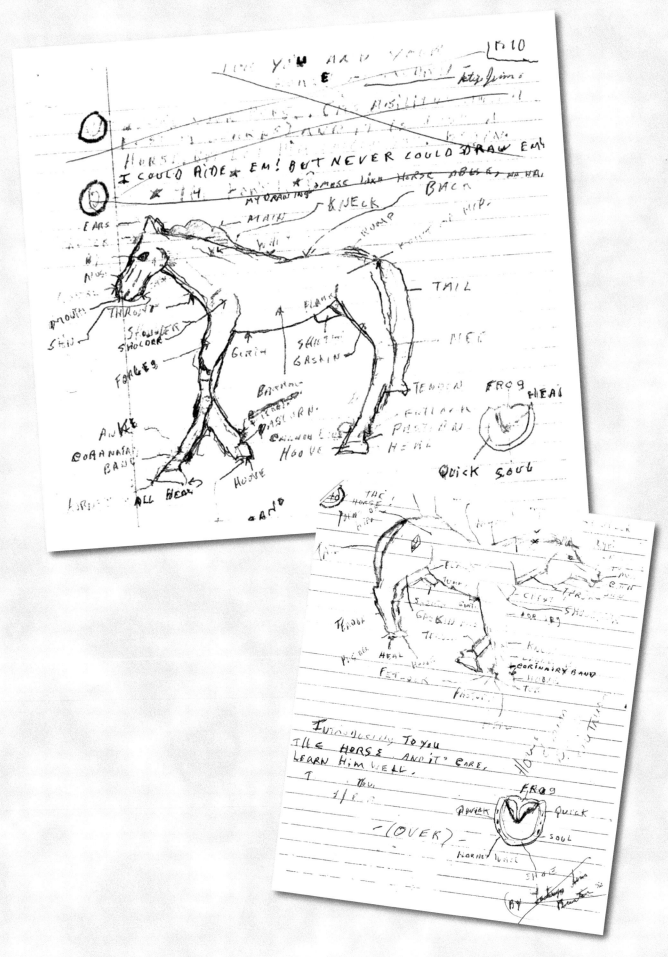

True friends leave footprints in your heart.
Eleanor Roosevelt (1884–1962)

Latigo Jim. & Rusty R.

True friends leave footprints in your heart.
Eleanor Roosevelt (1884-1962)

ON THE TRAIL
WITH
LATIGO JIM

Plumber Hill
Lookin S. from CA. Cr.

Signs says it.

CD. Cr. Farm, Main
Houses Shop.
CD. Cr.

Trail Head.

Parts of Latigo Jims ridin areas S.W. of Libby

Behinde C.D. Cr. Farm

Rode 4727 N.W. of Farm

ON THE TRAIL WITH LATIGO JIM

Jim Bunton and His Faithful Horse Rusty:

- ◆ 15 Happy Years Together
- ◆ Rode 38,400 Miles Together
- ◆ Jumped 257 Black Bear
- ◆ Ran Through a Dynamite Blast
- ◆ Two Gun Fights With Bad Guys
- ◆ Poked Deer Carcasses
- ◆ Raced Trains, Kicked Up Dust

Jim Bunton, Columnist 1989-1997 for The Montanian newspaper, Libby, Montana

Printed in the United States
By Bookmasters